OUT OF TIME

poems 1998

GW00703171

Jay Ram

Jay Ramsay is a poet, psychotherapist and healer in private practice. Project director of Chrysalis—the poet in you (since 1990) with its two part course by post, he is the author, co-author and editor of over 30 books. His passion is in helping people to connect to the creative spark within themselves as their primary and essential being which predates the adaptive self of our social conditioning.

also by Jay Ramsay

books & pamphlets

Psychic Poetry—a manifesto
Raw Spiritual—Selected Poems 1980-1985
Trwyn Meditations
The White Poem (with Carole Bruce)
THE GREAT RETURN bks 1-5:
The Opening /Knife in the Light—a stage-poem/The Hole
In the Valley of Shadow—a cine-poem-cum-fantasy/Divinations
transmissions
Strange Days
Journey to Eden (with Jenny Davis)
For Now (with Geoffrey Godbert)
Improvisations
Stories Beyond Words
Meditations on the Unknown God
Heart of Earth (bk.6)
Tao Te Ching (with Martin Palmer)
I Ching (with Martin Palmer)
Kuan Yin—the 100 quatrains (with Martin Palmer)
Tantrika—love songs of the Sixth Dalai Lama
Out of this World
Midnight Silver
like lightning inside lightning
Kingdom of the Edge—Selected Poems 1980-1998
Alchemy of the Invisible (with Genie Poretsky-Lee)
After Rumi
The Message (with Karen Eberhardt Shelton)
Chinese Leaves/Dream Whispers (with Genie Poretsky-Lee)
Via (bk.7—in progress)
Local Universe
The Heart's Ragged Evangelist

recordings

Thread of Gold (with Rosemary Duxbury)
Night Road of the Sun—Selected Poems 1987-2003
Alchemy of the Invisible
Anamnesis–the remembering of soul (with Tibetan Bowls)

OUT OF TIME

poems 1998 – 2008

Jay Ramsay

PS AVALON
Glastonbury, England

© Jay Ramsay 2008

First published in the U.K. in 2008 by PS Avalon

PS Avalon
Box 1865, Glastonbury
Somerset, BA6 8YR, U.K.
www.psavalon.com

Jay Ramsay asserts the moral right
to be identified as the author of this work

design: Will Parfitt

front cover photo: Jay Ramsay
back cover photo: Lara Fiedler
section photo: Carole Bruce

ISBN 978-0-9552786-5-5

CONTENTS

PREFACE

Out of time: both 'timeless' and 'running out of time'—both these meanings specific to our time, and suggesting a third, another kind of time at 'the End of Time' beyond the tyranny of the clock and the maniac acceleration that is our slavery to it. To stop, pause and linger (which is also the practice of poetry) is to enter and re-enter this state that we might simply call Present Time, but it does not by any means cancel or erase the past: rather it deepens it into a more meanigful continuum which poetry also demands. To really be present means also to be open to past and future simultaneously at the seed point that each moment is in its encapsulation: what is remembered and what is anticipated are then part of one thing, one being as any poem is: both actual in itself, and potential, uncertain.

Mysticism, with its evocation of the 'Timeless Moment', long before the Now became fashionable as it now is, has been my bedrock here and key to the expanded state of presence that all these poems refer to, and take place in: ' the real reality' as John Cowper Powys also named it and which is essential to poetry as I understand it. That is, poetry not just as something written on paper but alive in the living air all around us and, so, intrinsic to the experience of life itself seen and witnessed as something that is always both literal and symbolic, concrete and meaning-ful (imbued with soul and spirit, and our secret becoming).

All these poems, beyond *Kingdom of the Edge*, my last selec-tion published just before the millennium, move into this Out of Time realm where these simultaneous meanings of 'time' are all co-present as we face an uncertain future. But if the spirit of prophecy is still meaningful or possible when time has ended, or because it is beyond time and always has been, then where we're going to is deeply to do with where and how we are *now* in all senses, and the evocation of that is a story that poetry has always told best, and the poet in us (in all of us) is here to live.

for all we love

You desire to hear something new
but I have no news
except that love should renew you.
This commandment is the news I give you:
nothing is more known to you
yet nothing is more new.
—**Gilbert of Holy Land**, *early Cistercian*

The hours of folly are measured by the clock; but the
hours of wisdom no clock can measure...
—**William Blake**

I sleep and my heart stays awake
it gazes and the stars, the sky, and the helm
and at how the water blossoms on the rudder.
—**George Seferis**, *Logbook III*

A poet overhearing a conversation out of time,
must be his time's interpreter...
—**Vernon Watkins**, *Aphorisms*

How we imagine our lives is how we will
go on living our lives.
—**James Hillman**, *Healing Fictions*

Time becomes more and more dream-like. It's often only
possible to know something happened or somewhere
was visited by seeing the marks I made.
—**Kurt Jackson**, *Sketchbooks*

Change is not accumulative, bit by bit. Change
happens out of time, all of a sudden...
—**Geoffrey Windham**, *Usual Me*

This is a journey without distance, to the place we never left.
—**Tom and Linda Carpenter**, *Healing the Dream*

Prelude: Midnight Silver

FROM THE DEAD

1. *for Anneke*

Your last photograph—or the one we remember you by—
Smiling in your pink hood, flashing your white teeth
Broader than your tautened skin and greyed ageing hair,
Warrior: as you motored round the Arboretum...
Still, silent, on the window's broad ledge inside

And outside, in the garden, in a flash of light
A goldfinch at the feeder, brighter than coal tit, chaffinch,
Greenfinch—any of these

And then landing on the ivy clad wall, feet away—
A kestrel, for a full half-minute, perfect, alert

Your gay greeting cards. Four days on.

And all your dying gone, into this magic of colour
As if these birds had sprouted from your fingers,
Your poor fingers that were clenched purple
Your laboured breath that fought it to the end—

Warrior: your smile now as wide as Creation
As possible as anything
                         beyond the boxed bend of our minds

Where these birds, like you, are all zest and eyes.

2. *for Ted*

You are now
What you always were inside.

You come as a shower of light, a quickening
Beam of concentration around my crown—
At the very thought of your name, you can be here—
As I see you stretch your arms, free as an eagle now—
And you send your images and symbols direct
To her, in the sash of yellow round her belly
The half blue disc in her throat...
And the glowing red ammonite between her legs

You are present, gold, amazing
Ten times stronger in your radiance
Calling me to what is real in myself, too

The only thing that is in fact alive
That all our meetings prepared for: your passing

And to think that you'll one day all be there, my dear ones,
Leaving me here for you to communicate through

                                                   only

In the silence when you go, you go so completely
Out of reach of all our senses and imagining
You fly and fade like wingbeats, dissolving
As I wonder at your freer state

                       and where, and if you are—

Until I see, greeting me, the simple thought
That *because* of our unknowing, we expand here
This is where we can go, beyond, into It All
Like a vast dome of light, an endless sky

                                where you belong

That is just the other side of Nature
And the rising curve of this Gloucestershire hill,

Like the thinnest of veils, a crystal wall
Present in every living cell...echoed in birdsong

And then you're here again, with another name and form,
Coming closer and closer... and going as far
                                on your journey home,

As far as we go out of each other's minds

Erased into the presence of what walks inside us,
This body of light, clothed, naked in its armour.

BLUEBELL TIME

after my mother

1

'Bluebell time', you said, in a ray of sun
Ghosting the graveyard path through the trees,
As time stood still in that evening light...

And then later in the flowers I saw
That could not be plucked, picked, brought in
But had to be gone out to...in the wild

And as ever, your time ahead of mine
—the way ours is, when we can see—
Like a pathway from your invisible eyes

A pathway through the dream: I mean the one
We cannot help taking, the only way there is.

2

World time took over, cluttering the deep
With its dreamless daylight sleep of busy-ness
Before I saw them, and suddenly stopped, startled
Like the hands on a clockface where no clock was:

Here among the nettles—and so lustrous, blue
They're surreal: their cups veined blue to mauve,
Rising to their tight sheathed topmost tips
As I wade in, clear a patch, and crouch

And they say nothing, only
I must give them the time

Give *what* time ?
Your voice, your hazel eyes

The tan-brown river rippling among its stones,
Your body arched by the flickering firelight...

Give time to what cannot be denied.

3

Wild earth, just beyond our reach
Silence of touch and of meeting —a man
Who walks in nature and does not speak
Till he becomes the river inside him

Till he chances to take the step
Beyond his life—loosening the bands
That fettered his horse from its kicking gallop.

4

What is this ? Still not bluebell light,
There is a language behind all we say or speak
That is, as It Is...and they grow there

Their coming brings that light
That is the new dream of mind to go by.

Blue, deeper than the green. Blue like night
That is its own light, glowing

That beckons at the corner of your eyes
Until you turn to face it—

Until I meet the face behind your face,
And you meet mine.

5

Blue, Madonna blue—
Blue-pale, sapphire, the heart's breathing
Blue freedom in the space between us, smiling
Holding, cherishing and releasing—

And bluebell blue, jewelled, remembering
The magic that is lunar, the dream that dissolves
Away from all our grasping...

The grace of you seen
In a shaft of sunlight among the trees,
Where no form, or face or body was
Only your innermost being.

VARIATIONS

after Loop My Loop, 1991 by Helen Chadwick

Braid my hair bright
With my mutton grey tubes
This is my transparency, and yours
That you do not see me

I am woman: mortal flesh and ache,
Beauty and gut pain—
Not an image in your brain

You will never see me again
As you have.

It's too late for fantasies and lies,
Wake up:

This is my beautiful braid
Without eyes or breasts or thighs.

Can you love me now ?

+

Braid me into the body
Weave my light into the flesh:

I am meat-bright, raw,
Outside in

I am an embryo in the eye
Of matter.

Where mother ? Where lover now ?
These piss flowers are wedding cakes of snow
Isolated, laughter-frozen, absurd.

I am abandoned into the darkness

I am my other brightness now

But here is my testament:

And can you braid me into you
Can you find me in your gut of guts too ?

+

Braid, weave
And then the snake of it moves
Bright blonde hair and tract
Coiled, sliding arond each other

In love with each other
Beauty and her other

No penetration: no vagina
All sinuous weaving curves
Of invisible hips and thighs

All a dancer
With her red mouth on fire
Her red flower
Her red bleeding underflower

A woman's body is one,
She breathes the earth in
Through every orifice

She can feel a leaf falling from a tree,
So when she says *beauty*, she means it.

Can you see what it means
To see the light of everything
Inside out in everything ?

Then you will see
Into the liquid soul of what we are
That is not stardust alone
But star-membrane in every cell;

The matter we are is everywhere
In the living stream of its seed—
And all our ache for union is this:
To be in it.

THE STONE SHADOW

at the Ceim Hill Museum, West Cork

Your crone's face, parting the lace curtain
Your finger like a beak, stabbing, gesturing
Us round to your frosted glass front door
With its cracked white paint and sign
And rusted bell pull:

And then you're here: eyes smiling, hair lank
Hands filthy, fingernails uncut "Hello to you",
As you gather us us to this room like a basement
Stacked with its stone, all over the long table
Covered with handwritten tags, under bare low lighting
Your old front room turned cave, wild woman's lair

As you start your unvarnished patter
Reaching for the first polythene bag of proof:
"Now here's the Irish elk", jaw-brown, intact,
"Here's the mama—and look, here's the baby"
As we clothe them in flesh with our eyes, nodding
But it's only the beginning—

"Now what d'you t'ink this is ?" you ask
As you hand us a see-through plastic box
Filled with round rolled earth like grapeshot
And we've no idea. "Dinosaur droppings !"
Caught between awe and impolite laughter
As we turn to the mass of stone on the table'
On it, under it, everywhere...

As you reach for an ancient cleaver
With its rough handle and downward-driven edge
As you hold it...and then, with everything you lift,
It's as if your body has always secretly known it
As you show us the indentation on a stone
With your finger and thumb "like this, see ?"

A stone shadow soul, remembering
A woman remembering, sheer stone-cast survival
With knife-edge, spear, axe-handle and plough
As phantom professors hover at your shoulder,
Authenticating them, one by one

And it's true, this is where we began
With nothing at the ends of our hands, but stone
Stone and flesh, flesh-stone, wedded to it
Even scratching the stars on it: the Great Unknown
That wheeled around us from sunset to dawn
And season to season's equinox

And then it's not far-fetched: but as near as breathing
As you cup this mottled circle in your palm
And tell us it is the moon, and how
You stood outside gazing "and it was just like this"
The lines, the pitted layerings, moulded,
Mountains, valleys, the Sea of Tranquility
As it glows white-silver in our dreaming eyes

To think of it being broken and shaped
Held like a sketch book to be pencilled in
But with something far stronger and stranger
That lies at the pulsating heart of Creation

Muscled in man and woman, clay, rib, rooting, rushing
Ground to a fineness, rugged, raw, earth-perfect—
Under the blazing helium ball of the sun.

CONUINCTIO

for Sally

This crystal twilight.

That new moon,
                    etched in the shadow of its circle
Where the whole air is translucent like a screen
Above the misty valley ground beneath

Those stars opening out like a vast
    Inner smile above your head,
        Your whole chest expanding to meet them

As I wonder what signs will be written there,
    As we drift into this quickening wave of light...

And now, as I turn,
                    the moon again
In the shimmering aura of its aureole

Venus below it,
                    and over in the west
The spreading gash of salmon-pink sunset sky—
Its cirrus streaks scaled like fish skin
As they stretch and flare
                    over my head

Announce in language that is neither spoken or silent
The coming together of spirit and matter.

Journeys

IMPROVISATION ON FLOWER MOUNTAIN

Huashan, Shanxi Province, China

*'Connect with your inner silence
And the way is even and broad...'
    —at Jade Spring Temple*

The mountain rising
                    bone-white
                                with its green foliage

Through the last initial gate—

A pagoda stripped to two characters
Leading to the bridge

Over the foaming yellow-brown water below
As the train passes slowing behind...

And it breathes its brief freshness
As you fall in stride

Until we come to the barrier
Where they say the path is closed
With last night's flood, where a bridge has collapsed
Only amenable to your official note—

As we breathe with relief,
And the way opens again:

The great rocks swell in the river
Carved into being and graffitied in grace

Now the stalls are deserted
Only the cicadas hiss above the path-side stream

And the sunlight slants out
                                lighting the cobbles

Flanks of the mountain
                         exposed like smooth mud

                 dried to a clay finish

And now the stream water
                         oozing from the shiny black rock

Warm as a swimming bath
  Pure as its silk taste
    Dissolving through the tongue

In your mouth of quiet:

Great Huashan
Flowering in the haze
Above your sap of river water

Your roots impossibly deep
Your vertical strength
Like a heart exploding upwards

Holy Huashan
Transcending your stelae

And in this moment of a brown-winged butterfly
Your tao more luicid than language can ever be
Frothing round a rock

As a monk runs past me
Along the gutter line
In his red habit of a T-shirt
Clutching his shoes—
His gaze fixed forward

And the path curves round
Into the open throat of the river

'Whiting your mind out with water'

Where each syllable stretches
                              in its ocean-roar
And as broad
              as your arms can open

And vertical down the crevass
Down the centre line of your naked body, standing

As the gaps betwen the stones seem to widen—

And the sun's streaming is a silent song
Borne on the wind from its higher ground,

A song that lifts the air above your head
Beginning where your mind ends

Great Huashan,
Holy Huashan

A tiny golden throne for the pure light in you
And one for your sister too

As the way reaches a narrower gate
And the river roars higher—
                            and raising your eyes

A thread of spray like a rope flung down

As you breathe in under the acia tree
Where the butterfly repeats itself
Circling around you thrice

And the path levels the air like a wall

Then the rumbling of distant thunder
With its after-storm echo of more

And the one in you who is already ahead
Who has gone up into the cloud-mist

The one you spend your life looking for
Whose hermit's face is your own—

Or only outside you like some rare fruit,
A wrinkled peach of distillation

Where the air around him is gold
Even as he ages

His immortality in the invisible
In a far livelier communion of saints

That reaches you now as vibration, prompting you

As the path suddenly levels
                              easing into sand
Under a cloak of creeper

Then again, the thunder

And the way broken, ringed in a curve of stones
Where the cobbles drop away into the river
Narrowing by its muddy diversion
Where something else has fallen

The air weighing everything in the balance,
Like a hand holding scales full of liquid,
Scored with spirals...

And the essence of what is vertical
That translates into everything

Every circumstance, every chance

A blackbird's wings, startled away—
A green ladybeetle landing on your wrist
The path that knows what care to take

The thread
                from two hundred feet above

Floating down finer than lace

The tree-shrubs clinging to the sheer face
With its variegated stains
Of pastel and pale ochre,
Burnt sienna—

As a vast boulder opens into a postbox red door,
With a long chain dangling down among footholds
An ironic invitation—

A tiny window etched at the brow of its dome
As if we were only beginning
To get far away enough for silence

The boulders large enough, like the river's roar

As two rocks frame a gap like a diamond
And an old Taoist floats through from behind
As soon as seen, ghost-gone, with a smile...

And on the other side, a young man and his wife
Offering food: laughingly, gratefully refused

Leaving the backward look of love
That warms the air like lightning—

And in a deserted covered precinct
Under its ornate gabled roof:

A large empty font, in concrete
Its yin and yang hollow

An open well for the dreaming rain

A man in a blue shirt in the corner, fast asleep

The thunder echoing, rolling

As a group of young lads come down the path
Trying Chinese, then announcing in student English
That *the way is interrupted*, anxious, hurrying

The water in the gutter drain quickening
And then another rained-out shelter

The path steepening to its embrace

And you could die happy now
You could die in the daylight thunder
By the flooding gutter
With the path warming your knees,

The shelter swept through with a wild broom
Of river mud, caked round the narrowing steps
Among the crisp packets and melon rind

How puny our habitation beside these heights !

And how much all we have is like a way station
That a river in torrent can swallow in seconds

As the path lifts up like a ladder
And the choice to climb on
                              through your sweat

As the brown butterfly flutters by again

Come to your tao of breath
As you have to the fire in your legs

Walking at the speed you need to
As your mind suspends

No judgement: only the truth
Of the way at any moment—

The one you are inside, unvanquished

'Never born, never dying'
—you understand what it means now—

Forever born, forever dying
Into the Real Human flowering...

Narrow cut steps on the other side
Tantalizing, disappearing under leaves

You must quickly his passing face saying
The thunder repeating

North Peak lost in cloud

Fragments of collapsed stone
                    choking the channel—

The butterfly frozen on the step

A solitary yellow flowerhead
Reaching out by brambles

Beyond fear as the sun streams

As the path levels like an entry
                        into the light

A little narrow gate where no gate stands

Only an old couple waving white-haired behind

Where you press a wild yellow iris into a crack
In the path-side streaming rock

Before its white water hits you
In a cold menthol blast—

And you watch a fallen rock inching its way to drop
Suspended, forever about to fall
Until you realize
                        it isn't moving at all

The air roaring like a jet plane overhead

No Fear: this is the threshold

As three workmen appear from behind
Bare-chested, long shovels over their shoulders,
Nonchalantly walking on up ahead—no fuss
Past the broken stones and swept roots
Where you had decided you were going

Bowing under a little arch
The steps as they turn vertical

The way through the eye of the needle

A stairway to heaven, or bed
An attic of clouds without a mattress

Only a thin blue abandoned polythene bag
Like a condom discarded by a passing god

As the clouds part, revealing the blue-at-last-blue
And the peak like the tips of two hands making a cathedral

And where the broken bridge
                        finally shears away

This is it
      as the workmen hover, shaking their heads

Beyond belief
         as you point up a thin muddy track
Gesturing a loop away and round

Crossing the great water, now it's spent

As its sound falls away to birdsong
And the soft squelch of wet ground

A way people don't think to go
Under the bowed apple branches
In this Garden...

Where the track runs out into trodden weeds
And a bank above the river

To cross down walking on its boulder-bed
Where the air watches and waits, hanging

Scrambling up
        to where a young monk raises his thumb
And another grins, as they all gather round
In front of the small temple doorway

Laughing to speak with hands, fingers, figs, anything
Posing together as she shyly clicks the shutter

And then just as you leave, remembering
One phrase in your language that he knows

Happy Birthday ! Opening his hands

And as you round the corner
Where the steps begin again
What can be left ?

But the youngest, strangest
Most mysterious thing of all
There among the rocks and fallen debris
Where he stands holding a tiny plastic spade
His eyes widening wordlessly—who ? Who are you ?

Despite your greeting
You missed him

Only turning finally to speak as you leave him
Niha

Climbing as the tiled roof lifts from below
And the peak stands ahead

As slowly all the way you have come, like a life
Threads down as it opens below

You have come this far and what do you find ?

A rocky platform under the summit drenched in water
Two parallel staircases like soaked rope ladders
An edge that pulls your belly to itself

A place to finally stand

Stand and look back,
Stand and breathe

Being mountain, being man
Where the edge falls away

Bending your knees and lifting your arms
Until your breath becomes the air it breathes,
And you can feel the mountain through your feet

Being the message it brought you to receive

Like your friends below, waiting to greet you...

The waterfall that will cover your head—

As the rose light glows on the peaks
                              and your heart
                              streams open:

Huashan, Huashan
A mantra that is alive

A heartbreath and a message
In the invisible ink of its air:

Where no monastery, temple or gateway stands:
Strength beyond fear, it says

Strength beyond fear.

ROUND TRIP

for Virginia Tevendale , Ruth Marshall & Treasa O'Driscoll

1. *Green Song on the Liffey*

While the young man concentrates intently
On a mobile phone in his hand
As if it's just landed there out of the sky—
A green light, away down to the left, on the bridge
The same colour as his keypad
Is shining into the silver glittering water

And above the seething traffic
A three-quarters moon with its rainbow-tinged aureole
Like a searchlight against the scudding clouds...

And under the bridge, down to the right now
Its tunnel ceiling lit up in green

As the song on the coach proclaims
'If you want to move your mind, move your body,
Move your body...'

And then it's verdant

a green song

all the way down.

2. *In the Waterford Dark*

It took a long time
With the phone-in programme
The shrieking girls who'd won prizes
And the DJ's incessant patter—

And through miles of building site suburbs
It seemed it would never end—

Us in this bubble on wheels
And the whole of Ireland out there in the night

But slowly the darkness became stronger than the radio,
We entered a white world as rain became snow
Dusting the village rooftops
The tarmac narrowed to tyre-tracked traces

We finally came under the surface,
And I knew there would be silence

The driver asleep in his seamless bed
Snoring and murmuring through his dreams.

3. *Carrick to Limerick*

The light you stand in
As you wave farewell
Finally wordless
Like a golden vase—
A swathed mummy, alive, glowing...

At Clonmel, she comes onto the bus
Quiet-voiced, wearing glasses like a disguise
And a light black windcheater.
The driver clears a seat for her—
And she is a lover, she is Christ's
Without a habit, in her liquid grace.
We roll along in the morning light
Blue touching the edges of our eyes...

And then in an unnamed town
As the light gleams on the shopfronts and pubs
She slips off with a soft 'goodbye'
And as the bus draws away
Pausing briefly before the last one
In its deep rich red and yellow
The sign reads *The Crock of Gold*

A heart-stunned meeting in soul
With all its secret armour taken away—
As openly given as the day.

4. *North of County Clare*

What is the journey ?
It doesn't go in a straight line
Even if we drive on the right side of the road

And in the bright fluid river of your voice
It is a story that is always unfolding
And then it's losing the way
(Did you see that sign ?)
It is half a county and it's taken hours,
It is Ireland out of time.

And in the twilight it is promordial
Through the gateway of every hollow castle,
In a flooded lake-field where the bare trees branch
And among these gleaming slate-grey slabs of limestone
Packed like ice...where, as you quote him
'The soul is not in the body, the body is in the soul'
And it's in his eyes and bearded lips
As the centuries roll back, and our faces remain
The houselights flicker, islanded like candles
And men and women are still trying to understand each other
Across the same divide.

And in the night: we watch faces glued to pub TV,
And we come to the young animals of Galway City
In caps, T shirts, black stockings and leather—
Shouting across the lit park...in droves on the streets
Where you wonder if it's safe to get out your money

And where are we ? It could be Any Place
Where humanity is on the boil
In the putrefaction of its undoing—

And is it any worse or better, less or more ?

It is the night
Where we're travelling and there's still no room at the inn
For love or money, despite the plentiful signs
We're out of season, like the truth,
And we've no safe plan. So it's trust
Or panic, as it closes towards midnight—
Until it's a child who tells us where to go
And we find a human welcome and bargain rooms
The whole place being refurbished in the midst of it all—

A hard working girl at reception with a heart of gold,
And the little one's Dad serving behind the late bar.

5. *Ninety Minutes in Connemara*

Hummocks of great whale-like rock hills
Floating on an invisible sea—
Above these shining peat-black pavements
With their dug bog furrows, and limp bricks
Piled by the roadside...

Height and depth
Protected from any invasion—
Its rugged clear light etheric, as we drive
And suddenly your voice swings back to mind
With all its soft clear song, Martina, saying *You must go*
As we stood on that wooden bridge and you
Leaned back at the thought of it—
Spreading your arms on the hand rail: *Connemara*
As a light I hadn't known came into your eyes
That stilled the air as we stood in silence...

So where does passion go ? Where are you now ?
Somewhere in the Latin American heat, far from here,
And fourteen years older in your skin
And those rare blue eyes, still shining—

But no distance from my heart and the fire that longs to be
And the one who is ash inside me
Where it cannot match the light to a human face
But falls to emptiness, hard as it tries

It becomes these surreal dreaming hills
Which is what is left: and as we pull up now
By a wild west bar in the billowing rain-edged wind,
Two old red-faced farmers are sparring like comedians
Side by side, with their eyes only for the weather
And the young bartender is desperate for life
For his memories of a rave summer
As he insists on his utterly incongruous music
Fragile as he is, in the midst
Of all this wild singing beauty...

We toast each other with Irish coffees he's made
Lifting their cool cream heads to our lips
Draining the glasses to their last drop—
As you raise your eyes, for a moment
As she did on that timeless bridge
A stain of beauty that can never be bleached
Forever there—forever inside me.

6. *Book Ends (Galway to Dublin)*

a.
You pause at the headlines you're scanning
Your heads leaning towards each other
In the brief stillness as the page hangs
Girl of 16 planned school massacre
Your age, as you glance at one another
And if that wasn't bad enough
As you move the folded paper in the gap
Between the two headrests—
Car thief dragged boy to death
As you meet his eyes as if to say
Crass, silently—and without a word

Then as your stop hovers ahead
As suddenly, you disconnect
Smiling, at some shared lovers' joke,
Able to live your own life, surviving—

And I'm glad as the sun that slants briefly out
As it lingers in your empty seats, like lint
Where you've gone into your futures...

If only it would.

b.
Porous world, seeping in through every pore
The way the grey does into our eyes
And minds... the road drifting on by
Blended with ruins and brand new houses
—Yeatsian towers and New Age bungalows—
As the news is spelt out again with its cruelties
We look at the grey which cannot contradict it,

It is true: and the worst we can do
Is agree to it, in every thinking second,
Even as it weighs us down, denying that force
That lies buried like a fountain in its brightness
And sudden upwelling—

And that can break out in its true anarchic name
Anytime,

I was going to say in random acts of love
But you might be thinking rage, or grief—

The rain mists the rhythmic wiper-marked screen
Like a giant lidless eye

However we agree.

KIAWAH

for Katy Portmann, after 23 years

1.

This is present joy:
The sun sparkling on the sand
And on thousands of fragments of tiny white shells...

Sandpipers call above the waves—
And no thought beyond each barefoot step

                                in all this space
Only the light ahead, as you raise your eyes
To the sun that is feeding you through every pore

No future straining at the edges of your mind
But here under your chin where your heart opens
In an incredible pool of warmth

Where everything you could dream of
Is in its burning water

Where the sea salt smell spins you back across the years
To that sunrise harbour between the worlds
As the ferry's horn boomed—
She was arriving

Returning you here to the same placeless place

Where a worm hole in the sand erupts
In its tiny volcano of bubbling water
That is its punctuation

And the warm seamless wind takes it all

2.

She approaches from far across the sand.
You walk towards each other, but at the last possible moment
Veer aside—

She towards the waves,
You as if to leave the beach...

Then you watch her walking step by step in her own time
Down by the foaming edges of the water
Far down, almost out of sight.

And strangely you sit, waiting for her to turn
As you know she will: and when she finally closens
You stride down to meet her

For a split second
As you raise your eyes—as she does,
To an exact mirror of your unspeaking self
In the silence that surrounds
The precious space of her
Pure otherness.

You know it's not right.

Not a word spoken. Or even a smile.
Only the briefest touch that speaks it all,
Eye to eye.

You watch her walk away
Until her silhouette burns
Against the sun,

Slowly becoming light.

3.

The heart has its own timing
Out on the waves where the pelican floats like a swan
Before it lifts up into the wind

                    dropping
Like a rusty pair of scissors—

                 and before I see
There are two of them,
With the colour of the sunset sky

                      beginning to reach them

Two, where there was one

I and thou forever, when in my eyes
You become you

And now the horizon sky is as if full of them
Their etched pterodactyl beaks hovering

And then plunging into the moment
Where we are shocked open.

A SUICIDE BOMBER REACHES THE LIGHT

after 9/11

So where are the beautiful women ?
I have been in hell, where my heart could not breathe
flame racing down the length of the chassis on impact—
the last thing I saw as I buckled to my knees
the slit throat of the stewardess (the one I denied)
and even then, I knew...and then
the most unbelievable blackness
darker than I could have ever imagined
and soft as velvet, falling as I flew

Then the light like a sun came
from as far away as a single star...
and there are many of us, all moving together
and the light became white-robed figures
waiting as if at an Arrivals
and there was one for me, and I cannot tell you
but her face was pure love
and my heart seized—

I died again there in her eyes.
My mind flooded with that sunlight
then I woke. And all around me, the others who had come
being tended to, as I watch them
(one still holding his mobile phone)
in their soul bodies and their grieving
made of the same substance—and then I knew
where it all went wrong, and how
my future now lies with each one of them.

They do not speak Arabic here
they don't need any earthly language
these beings speak with their eyes, mind to mind,
and most of all, straight into the heart—
and this appears to be some kind of hospital

but outside, as in a field of white
and there is a path between two hills
where some are already walking.

I cannot recognize anyone, but everyone I see
is already familiar to me
you will probably not understand this...

As for you, Mulla Omar, you didn't understand anything
and the text you gave us is a lie:
there is no Prophet here, sitting in judgement
all there is is Love, and naked souls
waking out of their shock and pain
and loving souls who sit with them, and guide them:

All there is is Love—and what she says is
it can be mine again if I choose it.

THE BOREEN

It runs off a road off another one you'd call a main road if you
had to.

All the way past the tiny neighbouring farm to a dark green and
white repainted gateway, a silent swathe of pine trees lead in as
boreen becomes drive, past an old forever-beached wooden boat
filled with earth and rocks with a giant hogweed for a mast.

Walking past it in the soft suspeneded summer twilight, leaving
the fairy trees over your shoulder in the rising field, and down to
where it begins again

two paces wide, with its grasssed-over centre dotted with purple
vetch and daisies—and fields you've never seen so wild either
side, fields that go back to the beginning of time with their thick
green rushes and yellow ragwort

but wait: what can you hear ? Nothing but the air, nothing but
the flies: no car, near or far, no house, no dog past the
overhanging trees towards the little bending laneside glen

and you walk into a Silent World that was the world, the lost
world found, and you found in it now

flanked by its overgrown uncut verge:its waist high grasses sown
with *equisitum* (green horsetails from the beginning), bog iris
in its rising green blades, strawberry flowering brambles pink as
roses...

till every step becomes your breathing, where you are the only
rhythmic sound, the shod soles of your feet on its dove-grey
tarmac covering

as you jump—a disturbed blackbird startling your heart with
its warning cry, its wings lifting out from unde a tree, passing
through you—

and the tan brown coats of two horses grazing up to their bellies
in reed grass in their fine muscular bulk are as loud

in the silence you have come to, like your senses renewed again:
and you, animal-human, spiritual and mortal, Adam return-
ing alone all his life towards paradise, Adam without his name,
baptized again in the living silence that was the language we lost
that is all your body knows

and all that secretly breathes through it whispering your untold
being

that walks this boreen and to a place that is off a road, off a road,
off a main road calling itself Your Life.

Co. Sligo

'All by the light of a strange sun'

All by the light of a strange sun
where we know where we're going, or don't
but it's in the glow that comes
as we meet and exchange
rising up within your eyes

and the ground of your face

echoed in this winter light today
these days, of sun appearing and vanishing
leaving us in shadow, then brightening...
fine as a needle threaded in silver cloud
pointing the way without hands

where we're all interwoven as we're meant to be
and where the future is: these Advent doors
framed in azure possibility—
even as we're still bound to what we've been
living this moment of our lives, which is the mystery.

THE WEST DOOR

It hovers somewhere like an invisible curtain
in the middle of the M4, between junctions.
A double door, maybe, that can open both ways.
You have passed through it many times on your way to me;
when will you now ?

And as I ask the question
it swings open, into the symbolic
air that is also the real sunset...
because we don't know the time for love or dying,
dying or love.

Lao Tzu rides towards the mountain pass,
my father moves quietly through his latter days
and you are coming to talk to me about 'us'.

Maybe what moves in your heart will find you there
where the borderline shimmers like rain;
maybe you will be miles this side of it
before you realize you've driven beyond
without having to go back again.

In this kingdom where we live now
everything we do is surrendered,
everything is for love.

ON HARESFIELD BEACON

Everything is in God.

The day, the hour, the moment...
the sky stretching open as I drive
choosing to go to this height

Then parking in the crowded lane
in the cloying mud at the verge,
walking back to move the car in closer...

And still the moment-to-come preserved,
across the open heath ground
unmissable and unguessable, given,
you: standing as if rooted to the spot

your eyes staring, asking *Do I know you ?*

Pausing as strangers do, caught between
bemusement and a curious *deja vu*
I repeat my name. 'Again !' you demand
in your strident Dutch accent, as you explain

that this is how the stroke has left you
sometimes quite unable to finish a sentence
(having forgotten where it began,
suspended, open-mouthed, in the gap between)

so like a poem, that races on beyond
what the hand can keep up with
only to arrive breathless, and find it gone...

As we stop time now, standing
slowed down to this synchronous moment
each syllable spelt out (again, *R.a.m.*)—'*Ah* !'
as you grasp it at last, visibly relaxing

your voice beginning to flow in its channel
eyes sparkling grey, cheeks flushed apple-red
in the cold clean brightness, the intense clear
azure of the sky above us, surely heaven-sent...

And as your gift to me there, finally leaving
glancing over my shoulder to wave, as I walk on
taking the brief descending path on my quest
into the still deep-frosted woodland

to know finally
everything has its being in God
every moment, meeting, journey

where all we need to do is allow it,
letting You be...
                    there is our road

and no missing it.

SCINTILLA

for Anne Cluysenaar

Suddenly: at some point near or beyond midnight, when you've been driving for longer than you can think clearly, the real reality occurs to you—simply and almost overwhelmingly

that it is all happening at once, all of it: being born, dying, falling in love, parting...

grieving, killing, lying, laughing...

running scared, dancing for joy, screaming aloud, starving

                    ...as the veil tears

—all that has been held apart for the sake of sanity, clarity, individuality—

all of these brightly imaged scintillations like fragments of film gathering around a single point,
                    a single cone,
                              shining in this darkness

this moment, this *now* of reality that can't be uttered because it is everything—

                    seeing that

                    it can only be

          as all of us, finally, choose it

AT THE HOTEL LEUSDEN

As an exercise, imagine arriving nowhere
that is familiar: a hotel in the middle of Nowhere
your driver guided by a female voice instructor
her voice soothing, but firm. And the hotel
with no obvious entrance as you circle around it
finally entering up a half-hidden ramp; as if to a castle.
The reception staff courteous, a simple form to sign
with only your name required (the only thing
you have to leave behind). Then finding the escalator,
the 4th floor leading you down a coridoor
to your *en suite* room with its touch-button key.
And entering, a huge king-sized double bed
(that you later discover is two lonely singles merged)
with its gold and orange covering, desk, TV
and veiled curtained view out to trees, an echoing road
all filling its odourless void in the longed-for silence
as you spead out a few of your books and papers
and take out some of your crumpled clothes: what is it
that makes them look so strange and incidental
abandoned even, as they will be, disowned ?
You have at last arrived nowhere, where the Self lives
where you won't need anything, not even your mobile phone.

Central Holland

SWOON

for S.

A place of deep and sudden sleep, as unexpected. The landscape rushing past, become invisible.

Not even a high speed train...until it resurfaces inside a dry mouth.

Your eyes looking at mine, into mine, in this nick of time... across the dark brown table, hazel brown beryls edged below by lipstick, and a single deep line rising up across your forehead.

What is it like for you looking ? What is in your eyes behind your smile ? What is your liquid truth I can never quite see ?

This is the place, and we are in it without being able to say anything about it, or very little, so little in fact that we'd rather just go on looking.

Then is only the awareness of when we finally need to stop as the others arrive.

One place time, and in No Time. The birdsong outside in the rain wet garden, the french doors closed.

And as you close your eyes, it vanishes too, all of it...till the remaining thread of sense becomes attenuated, scored by phrases of music. Deep sleep takes you, loosening you from where you are again

till all there is this extinction of where you thought you were, that some of us call death.

Places

WAYLAND'S SMITHY

It does not feel like death here.

The beeches ripple listening, alive right through themselves,
Where the corn, shaved to its stalks, is ploughed to the edge
And the long laid knife-wedge of green
                              could almost be breathing

It's not a funeral, it's a beginning
A portal, a place of entry
as you stand, touching the stone's rim with your hand,
it's coming into the depth of your *own* life, that threshold,
and as you pause, you can see all the way inward,
and it goes on further beyond your eyes
and it's in the trees, the breeze, the rain dripping,
flowing deep under you, and all around you, in you

Life, deeper than we can see or name
only within reach of our soul-skin and being...

Let the god come:
He is already here
Breathing his welcome
In his wild man's heart.

            The tomb lies open. It could almost be a hearth.

And at the other end, as if at the foot of the bed, feet spread—
a giant could be lying with his arms outstretched—
on a healing table, now

But he has *given his head*, given it to his heart
at the open entrance where we can all see in
he has *given his head*, so that the trees remain,

            Like His Body, all over the autumn ground.

A TREE I KNOW

for Mario Petrucci

It stands in the dream by the gate to the fields
Its leaves full of whispering particles of wind
Where every leaf is an unwritten poem of air
Unopened, in its spell of hush

In sunlight or moonlight, shimmering in the dark...

And how can we fix it, paint, or name it ?
It holds us, as it holds the sea

In its mystery that is other, like you
With its broken mirror of leaves
I can't see myself in

So then it is a door—to the night or the day
Where our other voice speaks from inside the mist
And the sun, that is clarity to us

'I can only call it grace', you're saying

Where we can talk back
—and, who knows, to each other in the silence
Without even knowing—

At our separate desks, joined in the invisible skein of the air
Where we watch and pray.

And its leaves fill with seething air
Like an affirmation
Beyond the ending

As our eyes meet, pupil to pupil
Beyond the mere words we exchange

RAHEEN

for Virginia

Don't put the faith you have for God in people
You were told, walking in the woods above here.
It may be true. Let's say it is. And if you don't
What do you do with it ?

'Love one another' is the mystery
Because it means in spite of everything
It is the holes in the clouds we fall through
Like angels, back to earth.

It is the faith I have in God in you
That is the question.

Co. Waterford

ANYTOWN, STROUD: TO YOU

The air suddenly warmer as you walk out, leaving your sanctuary
the lights of the town glittering, valley-cradled below—
the moon full, cloud-clear—and the sky a lustrous darkening blue,
as you climb the road passing the lit insides of the houses...
and the woman in the late shop unusually smiles—
and a man on your way back winds down his window
grateful to be shown the way

You lift your eyes again to the hills and their rising wooded edges
and where the land falls beyond to the river and the sea
and the place is a jewel, like this moment—
you can breathe...

A chance conversation with a neighbour completes it
enough to go back inside, and continue.

Don't believe every blue evening
but if you don't, what is there to believe in ?

How else could your eyes reach
the miracle of another's in the dome of their sky ?

And how would you ever dare to meet
this ebbing sea of air reaching your feet,

How could you ever call yourself happy,
or even feel you might be about to be ?

Dream on, we need you—we all need you.

IN THE HIGH CAVES OF KEASH

Where is the heart higher than the mind ?
A hand holding gemstones—a woman's hand,
yours, stretched out for us to see
green and blue, black and gold, filling your palm

where you went back guided in a flash
to a crevice where one green stone had slipped
translucent as sea-worn glass,
and found them all clustered like eggs...

And it is placing them carefully back
in their sacred secret place
that matters as much
as the rightness enlightens us in its glow,

we stand framed in the big arch
the spreading fields with their lake like a mirror below
and you there with your necklace like bone
I could have loved 3000 years ago
before any of this was named
Cro Patrick, the Hill of Fairies, Knocknastoon

And there is your ex-wife you were hating
for leaving you embittered and bereft
you cannot forgive yet

and still your palm reaching open
where the miracle is a moment,
as the heart breathes again—

And all the way down, as you tell me your story
'it has to be healing in the end...'
you hold open the gate for us, and there

is a meadow full of chamomile flowers
carpeting the green in bridal white
the one we crossed, with our eyes raised to the ridge,
where its porous, pitted scarp is gleaming in the sun.

SPIRE

Had I ever seen a spire before,
had I ever understood ?

In Ballymote, walking back from Ross's
rounding the corner, there it was
vaulting into the twilight summer sky—

sharpened
to its vanishing tip

that is God

at the stillest highest point
above the crown
(as of your head)

flanked by four small spire-lets
like candles, minor minarets

in-spired, then

where breathing in
and breathing out meet...
and to breathe is to be breathed

and then the whole building
the whole of the visible world
leaping to that point—

and yet staying, poised

earthed, anchored, tangible

in an ecstasy of darkening blue.

Co. Sligo

INNISFREE

A sudden dip at the last bend in the lane
down where the concrete pier juts out over the edge
and the wind draughts towards you over the incoming waves
as you stand, in a blast of cool mountain-driven air—

There it sits, realer than a dream,
the greenest of secrets unto itself—
apart from its little wooden jetty
that says, or seems to say, 'you can reach me'

But there's no boat in sight
and no one to even ask...

And this is how close, and how far
the peace is where you're connected
through and through

And if I can't sit here in peace,
where there's no means to cross
and nowhere to rest
but the uncut tangled verge

I'll never reach it

and nor, my friend, will you.

Co. Sligo

IN DRUMCLIFF CHURCHYARD

Cast a cold eye
On life, on death
Horseman, pass by!
—W.B. Yeats, 'Under Ben Bulben'

Where the wind in the leafy sycamores rises
and the grey stone of reality holds its thrall,
in tower and grave

The sun withholds its brightness
for long enough for gravity to have its place

and then slants out in a single woman's
blonde-gold hair and transient shape
enough to say
all that truly remains of us
is neither here, nor set in stone

And there is all the unknown light
that fills our minds with its own
which knows
that coldness cannot have the final word

even as we pass through alone.

Co. Sligo

IN THE ABBEY GARDEN, DELAPRE

for Fionnuala

Through a gap in the monastery wall
with its thick stone blocks and triple ray flaring above
framing a blank page of air, where the tarmac path reaches
across a quiet stretch of garden, lawned with herbaceous borders,
even as the traffic still roars outside in its sea—
as we wander across, talking easily, and down

—into another gap, unseen
between two long empty white greenhouses
where a vacant bench waits—and behind it,
inlaid in the brick, like a slit wound
revealing another skin that isn't raw, but dreaming...

this naked surprise of her

where she lies, on one side,
her right arm reaching across her brow
hand limp at the wrist, cupping her left ear
behind the waterfall of her hair flowing away behind her:

A cat poised on her raised left shoulder, paw curled by her throat,
the other paw reaching her heart, above the bared
gently leaning round of her breasts

and her left arm reaching, resting down—hand splayed
veiling the lower half of her virginity—
her left leg half-raised and crossed
where another cat wants to clamber on...

And if you think she's inviting you in, look closer:
her dream of silken watery abandon also needs this
inviolate privacy of her being
(as another cat appears between her knees)
as her hand says *No Further* now
even as your hand may touch her, caress her,

but not her beneath, as if under glass,
where the bricks curve and follow each molten line

fired harder than clay
unweathered beside their daylight counterpart
and that can't be defaced

even as her breasts bear a single scratched mark
like a scar: no hammer blow, no graffitti paint
something stopped you in your tracks
however your mouth may have smirked or spat

we call it beauty, grateful only that
the world cannot forget—
beauty

spelt over and over, silently, again...

And as we walk away over to the right, we find them
on a single brick pillar, together, embracing
behind the unflowering green, in the corner of the bed

thighs loosely joined between each other's,
arms wrapped, intertwined, turned heads blending
so that, as we stand side by side,
who is who, and who is male or female only ?

And half in the shadow of the full-leaved beeches,
where the high cracked wall has been climbed
and their monument, you tell me, pushed down

still they stand, martyred to the daylight—
as we do, in the heart of our lives
joined in that inner skin that is our body's breathing

to tell us that every loving kiss is holy
and every lover's body is our prayer

ANGEL OF THE NORTH

Astonishing the air—
wings-up alert as if just landed
out of the invisible's so much greater realm

and yet rooted as only presence can be
dwarfing the small hill become its base
above bushes in their sunlit spring-yellowing blaze
set against blue sky on this postcard...

And then who are you, bird-man, with your faceless face
your wing-struts stretched as wide as a jumbo jet's—
and the androgynous line of your body
rippling into solid merged gale-withstanding feet
where the weathered steel becomes wood so nearly breathing ?

In one pair of eyes, for as long as it takes
to begin to absorb the amaze of you, I want to say
you are more purely here than we may know
not only created and cast, winched and hefted, inch by inch
but as a Being in the guise of the earth
and all our folly you stand beyond, transforming it
in the standing shape of your vigil

—as the road swings, as the camera pans,
in the flight of any bird's wings, around you—

and not as crucifixion now, but witness
to the greater world you announce that never leaves us
however ridiculous we are
waiting and waiting for us to awaken
and scale the hill-mound's tiny distance to you, for always.

IN THE NORTH OF SWEDEN

for Lina Tegner

The darkened woodland, already past twilight
the exhausted horse, and you
—suddenly missing his footing, sliding to fall—
and either the pommel of the saddle, or his hoof
smashing blindingly into your forehead...

And unconscious as you were, you came to
all you knew was you had to get to the river
(although how could 'you' know ?)
and lay your head in the snow, to stop the bleeding
or you would have died there as easily
as it sank to 30 below

So you crawled,
but as if from above your body
and then as suddenly
I was everywhere and in everything,

you say
              as you tell me now
eliding across nearly forty years
your grey eyes and long blond hair in the candlelight,
as I close mine again in the frame of your face
imagining

...and somehow they found you
the horse found his way back to the stable
and they followed the tracks out over the whiteness
and the 16 year old came with his tractor

and you say
There was a crack in my skull, you know
and it was as if something else could come in

as you hands pause and your face shines
with a light any other light can only echo
as my eyes stay widened, seeing in some way
as you must have seen

reflecting this strange gift that is yours back to you
my fingertips itching for a pen
as you say

There is no other side. It's all here all of the time

in the light of our unknowable being,
where we know.

from **Island of the Sun**

Malta & Gozo

NIGRET

SACRED HEART: the ceramic house placque says
and then, only a few yards down
behind the slit of a grey metal
sliding garage door
a topless blonde with unzipped jeans
stencilled in black on a pick-up's polished steel bumper,
its owner lurking in the shadows...

So what is sacred ?
Mary as she raises her eyes
out of a cornice high on a villa's veranda ?
Two old nuns carrying a cardboard tray of veggies between them
stout as the salt of the ground ?

The question hangs like an empty mouth

When out of nowhere, or perhaps the future,
appears a battered blue dust-streaked Cortina
big white letters emblazoned on its rear window
like solidified cloud

POWER
OF
LOVE

it proclaims—

And the car, parked up beyond the garbage wheely bin,
With its registration KAN, and (we hope) here to stay.

GIGANTIJA

for Genie

Whatever this was, you do not enter here lightly
the worn holes at the threshold, empty as they are
bar your chest with air, as you look down
to a hollow depression in the stone
where you would have washed your face, at least

Only then, and inside
alcove after alcove, all you can do is piece
parts of a suggested jigsaw into a ritual
chamber after chamber of its mystery...

Only, as you reach the deepest part
do you find your heart strangely opening, widening
then again as you return to it...

And it's only when she tells you
what no sign or guide is telling you,
that this temple
is a map of a woman's body

that you understand
why you waited there,
where the womb is—

why your words fell away

and why you don't need to know
any more than you need to speak

as if it wasn't enough
to be able to walk inside a woman, and see
that you are walking on holy ground
that every holy war has since defiled

then you will know why
its great lips are sealed

CALYPSO'S CAVE

The way there is a garden
at the cliff's height, past the sign
by its arch entrance, in fading black letters
that says SEE (you maybe
didn't even notice—)

Geranium and cape sorrels
quivering in the light, wind-ruffled.
The way is a garden
opening onto a the cliff's edge
with its merciful grey railings,
sheering back from the eye's plunge
down to the dotted figures on Ramla Beach
and the turquoise sea...

The air is strangely sweet
as if with wind chimes
the calling song of a woman
without words—or need of them

And there is a crack in the rocks
you might just miss, to your left—
you could even fall into it, if it was dark,
and there

the uneven smoothed steps descend
polished by centuries of feet,
and a man in a blue peaked cap
with a wooden tray hung round his neck
offers you a cheap candle

If you're lucky, you can go down alone

And there on the cliff-cave wall
as you reach for a handhold,

HONEY it reads, in black paint
(or MONEY if you misread it—)
Honey for sale, though you can't see any...

At the cave's mouth, boulders screen the sea
as it opens inward, and you bend
into a small cavern of listening
(what was her song ?)

but still the opening reaches deeper
into a hollow cavity of darkness
and you wonder how far, and what
black shape might leap out or fly
bat-crazily out of your own fear

and is it a vagina, or an ear ?
All there is   silence   you glimpse it,
humming

as you stoop in further, holding your light
leaving the voices fainter above you
and as you reach out your hand, to where
the stone becomes as if moist to the touch

with what appears to be red and white quartz,
you realize it is coated in layers of spilt wax !
Ear wax, then, smoothed like skin to your fingers
as you pause, and a final chamber opens

It is an ear—you see it now
and you are crawling inside it !

Once more to where you can sit up,
and there, as you close your eyes
the silence under the earth can fill you
and you may come to know what she knows
as her lover from the sea lies asleep...

That there is honey in the earth
honey in the silence under the ground
and if you close your eyes
(go on, close your eyes)

you can hear, and smell, and taste it, now.

MDINA

I want to walk in the Silent City
watching your shadow walking with me
holding your hand without needing to speak
our silence full of our speaking.

Street after parchment stone street lit by gold lamps
alleyways too narrow for cars—
sealed doors, shuttered windows
and around every corner, another street
leading half into shrouded darkness.

To walk with you, holding your hand
in a city that has no traffic and no hoardings
step by step, where you can hear your breathing,
is the most intimate thing I can imagine.

I want to walk in the Silent City
holding your hand, and walking freely
speaking or whispering what we need to say
our silence full of our listening.

MARSAXLOKK

In the moment that is seeing:
these boats, in their bright stripes of colour
in the mirror of the harbour water's rippling moving
red, blue, white, green and yellow on their sides—
prows signed with the ever-open old Egyptian eye

as water calls to water, my eyes begin to swim,
my forehead opens inward, enfolded,
time freezes...

and I am six years old, sitting
in the chamber of our dining room
at its dark stain-polished table, its walls
papered in strips of red and gold, gazing

up at a painting of these same boats
beached in a line, wondering at their design,
and why are they here ? What do they mean ?

As unknowing of the future as it already is
waiting in time for us to arrive at it ?
This standing here, still answerless,
as they bob in all the rainbow colours of a life
shored like the shells of strange journeys, returned.

ISFAR

This is where the love cars come.

High on these cliffs in the wind
poised in their bubbles
where the land sheers twice towards the sea

the air ruffling these tiny irises
peeping among the loose scree at the edge—
where you walk, and it opens into a hairpin lane
threading down into the strips of field below.

Sealed doors in the cliff. Old window openings.
Where the sky meets the sea. Far and near

The observatory perched like a mosque,
with its white dome reaching into the unknown...

And the sun like a moon, pale pure gold in the haze
hung like a veil, as we sit, its radiance diffused
into the yellow of these spring-flowering
giant fennel on their stalks, everywhere below
threaded together in light, in a web linking everything
and the clump of bright gorse-gold flowers at the rim
of this great wedged boulder between us and the sun
is far

Near and far. So near and yet

What draws you back to gaze into any distance
that is the space of the mystery we yearn for

beyond what we can see or know

note: Isfar in Maltese means yellow

THE GOLDEN ROCK

Here on a sandy beach become a shelf of stone
as if placed by a huge deliberate hand
—rolled downhill in bone-crushing thunder—
this sand-gold boulder, like a giant full stop
with all the expanse of sunlit sea beyond
in this bay which means 'Little Garden'

As it hangs on its precipice, in far away Tibet
painted gold all over where it is poised forever;
and here it's mutable, airbrushed by wind and sun,
scored (as you come closer) with fig-sized circles
of vaginas, and graffitti names already fading
blurred, the oldest almost indecipherable
PALMILLA...and was it Toni, or Janice ?
and the sand-covered face of a hooded alien
carved in laughter, become the ghost of a smile...

as cell by cell, rain wind and spray erase them
as from the surface of a mind, so that this rock
that could also be your anchorage
is constantly becoming where it came from
out of the high womb of the globingerinous cliff

golden as its gift to our eyes, and the sea.

AT GOLDEN BAY

1.

The world below in the wide bow of the sand
facing the sea

and nothing more between us, only light
nakedness, humanness, laughter and peace

Imagine. And it is already here,
heaven's gold is pouring down...

The sealed watchtower on its height is silent,
the pillbox beside it become a weekend retreat

and can peace overcome us like this ?
It is only who we already are when we're free
of being who we thought we were afraid to be.

2.

We take the tawny golden path as it descends
above the beach, then curving inland
levelling before it climbs again.

The afternoon hangs on fire.
Summer's reign has come.

And there, hanging
impossibly suspended
above the blue clay cliff face

is where the golden rocks come from:
one already slipped, slithering, stopped half-way
and this one poised to surely bounce right down to the sea.
All it would take would be some heavy rain.

All it would take that keeps our world turning...

A hundred and fifty feet below
a woman stretches out under a beach umbrella
more or less exactly underneath it.

And the path becomes sun-dried clay
cracked thin to its crust
rising to its lip before its crumbling scree toboggan slope
plunges down to the other side again

And you went down on cardboard on your *potata* !

Six big boys pace past us swearing
as you translate
'If you fall off here, you'll land in Mjarr !'
'It's true', you say, and it's only a game

And we could be in Utah or Arizona
at the height of this bared outcrop as we pause
Gjaena to our right, the Bay below

as we linger, a little group of strangers
always with the choice to make
drunk with sun, or secret hate.

RAMLA

1.

He stands there, baptized in sunlight and sea
and smiling laughter, glistening
in his wet yellow-gold swimming shorts
where the waves are breaking in the wind
playing with his son—small as he is, but large enough
to wade with him in the shallows, and run back
to hold his Dad's nose as he sits, and push him
back under the next wave as he squeals with delight !

And we watch them, on the beach's free TV
in timeless time, untiring as they dance
and as they finally walk away down the sand
there goes the future, a little man
who will feel the ground under him
walk with love and pride
with his heart open to life, baptized
his father inside him that he'll grow to, and past
this same remembered moment of joy ?

2.

She sits on the gold sand in her dark bikini
dark glasses and olive-tanned skin
her daughter laid across her, asleep
as if still at her breast, although it is a memory,
her four year old hair hair falling behind her,
rocking her gently from side to side
glancing up at the sun, shielding her eyes,
and then down again, at her self-appointed task,
so completely absorbed in this moment of her life
that nothing else could conceivably matter

even if one day it does, even if she leaves this
version of herself behind her like a skin
she is here now where nothing separates her
from her eyes, her breathing, and her arms
holding her daughter, who will be able to dream
as she sits, in a reverie of the breeze...

3.

It whizzes full of its wind-whistling
fitfully, crazily above us
like a large tricoloured surf board
let loose on a kite string—

as it darts from side to side, then rises
and as abruptly, disastrously, plummets

then we see him on one knee on the sand
holding both strings down with the full force of his arms
to guide it as best he can
and stop it from swooping, sword-like
onto our heads as we leave the beach for the cafe

where we watch its writhings in safety
as the whole sky hangs on its thread above us
and behind it, the three ships
these elegant thin wooden schooners
with their white masts and decking above white hulls
exquisitely rigged and finished

motor out silently, one by one.

THE RIPON JEWEL

at Ripon Cathedral, for A.

1.

Glimpsed across the green December fields
a flag-flying castle, above the trees...
until you realize this house was built for prayer and peace.

2.

The briefest glimmer of light from the road
through a tiny window in the door as we drive on past
enough to say the building might still be open.

3.

The first exclamation of the nave
with its soaring, timbered, ship-bellied roof
its avenue of arches framing luminous gold

4.

The jagged zig-zagging silver glittering flames
on permanent display, by the Lady Chapel
inviting us to worship in an Age of Lightning—

5.

The carved varnished choir seating
with its cupped glass candles and rood screen,
the high altar with its mass of figurines
poised between glory and plastercast...

6.

The open doorway of the crypt descending
into a scratched limewashed passageway

to the niche, where the holy of holies
is an absent Resurrection

7.

Your face lit up by the Christmas tree
with its cut-out white doves dangling,
the one beside it hung with accompanying angels

8.

Your eyes alive in the final tree behind
filled with its radiant spangle of stars
as far as the eye can see, within

9.

And what else is the jewel but this moment,
alive with life as it is ?

Each fragment banded in gold
its roundel inlaid with coiled rope thread
each gem section unpolished, as it is

the quadrants marked
as in a Celtic Cross
the rest set, approximate, uneven

all that remains
of its once lost splendour
perfect in itself, as it is—

and as you, inviting me out now
to gaze up at the stars above the rooftops

as far beyond the neon haze as we can see.

MERCURY

in Boroughbridge, N.Yorks

There among the piled hymn books
kids' gaudy drawings and the panel displaying
the building's history, an oasis in a sea of stupid wars

—a naked man !

A great square of darkened stone edged like a brick
and raised up, half-hidden in a corner

where the slate grey twilight swims
and the display sign reveals one of his names

a naked man rising up out of its centre
laid like an open coffin

a naked man from the depths of time
who can only appear under the brightest light
flashed in its momentary blinding white—

exposing him: light, agile, beautiful
perhaps once with a headcrest and winged feet

Hermes, Mercurius, Mercury

and now simply naked, as he or she
in who you also are, to your surprise

shadowed in all you secretly need
in the mirror of your eyes.

FOURTEEN LINES FOR BRITAIN

Re-imagine this island, once called great
not merely motorway-scarred, a broken mirrorscape
but as a beginning of what we must become
if we are to live as one world people—

and we are its molten confusion, fired to ash:
smutty news, broken schools, littered roads
our heads held low, our hearts afraid
under the parade of all we are supposed to want...

But raise your eyes—and your glasses, friends—
where the fantasy fails is where life can be as she is
and Albion can rise, phoenix-like again,
buffed bright as a wind-filled spinnaker

our hope, where we live—in every village and street,
in all we can do for each other, and the God of Love.

from DIARY (IRAQ)

coda

for Ali Ismael Abbas

In the eyes, no recrimination
only the even gaze of a question
no one can begin to answer...
outsized, like brown beryls, looking up
the lips full, beautiful as he is,
his lustrous black hair recently cut
resting on a favoured pillow, with its flaming tulip
beside his right ear—his sister's ringed hand
poised, withdrawn from smoothing his brow

...the bandaged stumps of his arms, blown off
he wakes to, at every other moment
as the nightmare of pain continues,
their perfect use still inches from him
his blistered chest like a terrible painting
coated in layers of cream...the squalid
children's ward like a manger all around him—

No room at the inn for Love.

'It would be better if poor Ali died' says his doctor
but he lives to gaze at us across the miles, across time
where the soul knows no distance—
stretched on the helpless cross of his bed
with Mary behind him weeping
still asking us *why* ?

13.4.03.

Day 365

Liberator become oppressor:
two sides of an emotional coin
as slippery as grease in the palm.

A people pulled apart in all directions.

A wound constantly re-opened
before it can heal over:
crucifixion without end.

Counting the days, till when ?
And as many suicide bombers
awaiting a rude awakening in Paradise.

'We must not abandon this historic struggle'
proudly declares our Prime Minister
(wishing he was Churchill—)
and in the same breath, the next conscript
strapping explosives to his empty chest.

Let go of war ? As inconceivable
as the President abandoning the White House.

And the reason remains dark
it flows like blood under the ground
blood that everyone needs
but not human blood.

It only drives machines.

Hatred makes machines out of us all.

One small step
into the Kingdom
when we see what we are fighting for.

It means we must connect
must talk, must listen and express
must agree that ceasefire is the only key.

It means we have to pause.

The machine stops. It is switched off.

The way is clear: we fight for oil
under the guise of morality,
or we bow to the Earth's command
to live by a new integrity.

Oil, or human blood.
Hatred, fear and revenge—or love.

One giant leap

out of Hell.

Easter 2004

IN THE CHAPEL OF THE HIGH CROSS

in St Mary's, Porlock

Climb up to pray, that's right
Climb up to the high heart
Between you

Not too great—a compact space
Where you can be as warm
Together

A little space is all you need
As great as in your heart,
All the high cross means is there
Opening as the Rose in time

All it means
To reach your highest

Pray for that: to be royal in heart
Red as ruby, fine as gold
A free spirit that can never be sold

Bound only to love
That is for the highest.

MARATHONISI

Zakynthos, Greece

1

Rising, its spine lifted in an upward moving graph
its uneven triangle of chalk-white limestone—
sessile trees miraculously clinging to its sides

its name resonating like a mantra
meaning a long day's journey through centuries,
a journey without end in the heart ?

The anchor chain runs out into turquoise blue water
crowded with small craft

magnetized to its larger sea cave opening
as if to a fairground ride...

shouting, echoing voices as another is swallowed
briefly by harmless darkness

And despite them
slipping into the fish-laced, deep water
your blonde head bobbing seal-sleek beside me
as we breaststroke towards the smaller one

a mere lip in the sheer cliff's underside

its silence slowly coming to meet us
the sea turning milky jade in its shadow

Then suddenly shallow enough
to tread ground in, tread
pure white gravel-shingle under feet
as we lift our leaden-dripping nakedness

wading ashore under its overhang
stooping in under its ceiling of angular
coagulated plaster in fantastic shapes
stalactite-like bulges hanging down

and hidden in its far-left corner
coated with a dust layer, melted
into a parallel seam of rock—
crystal, in a mauvish striation...

Cave-church as it seems,
and so a place to cherish a sacred stone
picking among them where the wavelets lap,
their white-gold smoothness veined as if with hair
traced under translucent skin...

And everything so clean and clear as we stand here
fresh from its innocent beginning
the tubby, rumbustious Greek children
like their ancient ancestors, playing and discovering
before their parents' call from the mustard motorlaunch
interrupts their reverie, and mine

And we finally re-enter the water
amphibious, breasting turtle-slow, back out towards
our Ariel, and the busy distracted light.

2

No habitation here, only one tiny church
he's saying from behind the silver light wheel
gesturing around the other side of the island—

A ruined chapel where the wind blows...
but intact enough
to stop its profiteering owner
from building a hotel

to lure exclusive tourists

when nothing could seemingly stop her
this little forgotten shell did

the Church claiming the island as its own
the island claiming itself for itself, if it could
the Church having finally got something right
for the first time in 1300 years:

honouring the Creation, heaven on earth.

ST. CHRISTOPHER AT HAILES

in the church by Hailes Abbey, Gloucestershire

1.

He is the first in this church of riches
with its yellow brown tiles, gold altar cloth
and whitewashed walls that dutifully interred
an entire illuminated world, glossed over—

You draw your breath as you step in;
the still afternoon sunlight suspended
on the length of this weatherstained plaster,
and who is he ?

Standing twelve foot at least, giant
the unmistakeable shape of the head
centre-parted hair and trimmed beard
holding, what ? A bulging bagpipe-like
wineskin creched across his chest
and beneath

his midriff dissolving as if in water,
then his knees reappearing...

and the child he is carrying
becoming 'as heavy as the world'
as one child who could save us all

a child older and younger than time
who has kept his root in Paradise,
known by all Children of the Light.

2.

Did you know the story ?

Christopher (we are told) was a giant
perhaps meaning simply a very tall man
who ached to serve the greatest king in the world.

We may suppose his intial motive was
ambition, or sheer naivety ?—or both.

He meets a hermit who preaches to him
about a very different kind of king
urging him to live on the edge of a river
a very dangerous, fast-moving river
and to help folk crossing it.

The River of Life, we might imagine.

And there, was he waiting for a sign ?

He was living as we all are—
without quite knowing why.

Then one day he's carrying a child in his arms
above his waist, above the current
and as he puts him down on the other side
someone grows as tall as him—
someone is meeting him eye to eye—
someone with light all around his body

and who is saying to him: *I am as you are.*
Christopher, carry them as you have me !

3.

A prophylactic against the worst fate:
sudden death without confession...
seven hundred years ago—and now ?

A giant cradling a child, any child, in his arms
this saint to travellers, who is all of our fathers,
the good father we may never have known—

and larger than life, come back to remind us
that it's only by daring to cross the great water

that we find our true way home.

SHAPWICK

on the Somerset Levels, for Lara

1.

Turning off the dyke path
along the line of the old railway track
invisible now, under telephone wires,
here it is: where the reeds spell hush—
bleached corn-gold through the longest winter
mirrored in the peat-black of the water
(where woven Noah has sunk forever).

Two saplings among them
like a threshold, reflected: above and below
—you and I alone, and the birdsung silence.

Rounding it to where the Sweet Track is signed,
the black water opening into its sky
reed-filled, tall, the meniscus quivering
as if with anticipation, disturbed
by the restless skidding white water-fly
(the unseen fish twisting between his eyes).

Sweet Track pictured between the reeds
reaching back into imagined Paradise—
the way now beside a length of black pipe
draining its excess, waterlogged fertile depth
coiled to rise, under the leaning sanctuary trees

Bog iris like tongues of green flame
out of the pixelated pea-green water
glass-green, frozen in time

But not your feet, brown shod
under your brown cords, earth-honouring;
our footprints in sodden peat-grass, hours old
we sidestep—

and beneath your steps, your other self
warm, dreaming, naked, pelvis
pressed back willingly into the mud
as the blood gathers there...
to make love with the earth, how simple.
How fertile...sweet...forgotten
on our raised Slumberland altars
to no God and no harvest.

Bullrushes with their stalk heads
of mottled wool like sheep's, to ignite
burning spears in the encircling firelight,
as you look for signs...
What will it be this time ?

Down to our right, dry greying grass
gestures the back of a woman's head,
hair highlit with corn-like ears. Primavera,
even ageing, with Spring's blessing,
forever ressurrecting
                                    like you
autumnal and ageless, woman and child

And the birdsong all around
in all its threads: sweet chirruping chaffinch
the whirr of a squawking pheasant
blackbird, robin, and myrtle thrush in between

As we come to a little wooden bridge
and you whisper breaking the silence
only to show me
how the green water reaching away
under the branches
seems to flow uphill

here where anything is possible
shown as imagined

And trees out of reach of chainsaws and graffitti
live and die where they will
downy silver birch, hawthorn and alder
some leaning, some caught collapsing
bent like arms towards the ground—
some snapped off near the crown

as you gaze down again
at where the green pixels part
and the dark obsidian water opens again
in its underworld, underglass

and I love it here
as I love you
in your ground, in all
your depth and moisture

fecund, yes—earnt
a hundred times over...

As their honking cries approaching lift our eyes
sounding just ahead of them
spanning the soft grey air as they clear
the treetops, passing low, staying close
to the ground they love too...

as your hand reaches out to touch
the bark of this silver birch
knotted with thick-veined tree ivy
your ringed fingers and fur cuff
Iron Age and now, timeless in this silence,

and if I lean my cheek against it
all I can hear is the sound of bees
beneath the lightest breeze...
so that's what I will do
for as long a sit takes
you to compose it
                    in your digital window

both of us unselved in each other,
a man and a woman hollowed out by silence
into this economy of gesture—
the relief of No Words
allowing everything to be, and to be seen,
present, nowhere else, at last
breathing out...and then the slow

arriving of joy because
we are nowhere else but here,
in this Reserve for Human Beings
remembering who we are again at last

and then far beyond, rising
above the dry reed grasses, on the horizon
the Tor, with its towering I

and all of Avalon's water
spread like a womb around it

the Tor and its future
rising above the Mother
the only fixed thing
hollow in its naming.

Yellow pollen-edged willow catkins
lightening in your fingers
the dark of a farmer's deathly gun
shooting crows beyond
as we stay strangely calm.

And one fallen birch trunk
leads across the rhyne bank
to another rising above it
—and all that's fallen and changing

even as the depth remains
opening in each mysterious pool

where the willow branches become roots
reaching out of sight
                              and you
deeper than any single image
in all your changes, rising and falling,
like a memory of one
becoming all she can be

and the one you've always been
I can glimpse and feel in
blindsight and lovesight
but who is always deeper
than the water of my eyes

And as we come to the Decoy Hide
this is our desk, finally
by the raised wooden flap, at eye-line
and its vista of breeze-raked water;
Tor in the distance, eco-bars between us,
and the testimonies of all who've been here
inked over a broken hardback's lined pages
in gratitude, awe, playfulness and laughter.

Two gadwalls, two swans: two of everything
and in the falling light, circling round
as our silence slowly thaws to speech again
the wires hung as if with dream catchers
(to warn off low-flying birds) and baubles,
triple-lifesize gold Christmas tree baubles !

and a cloud of mosquitoes above our heads
escorting us, dipping and rising, to the gate.

THE INVITATION

Culbone, near Porlock Weir, N. Somerset

In the church at the bottom of the world
where there has been church for 1000 years
is the silence at the depth of your body,
deepening like a shelf reaching under your heart
where the densely wooded valley slopes outside
and steepens: uninhabited, unspoilt, unpolluted
as you walk on its high paths above the dreaming sea
shelted by the leaves' green canopy like an animal...

And where the stars shine as you've never seen them
white-clear as pinheads, clustered thick as trees
with the white dust of galaxies beyond, between them,
so that the universe itself seems a different place
as you lean back against a gravestone, gazing;

And now the morning birdsong tells you the same—
we are part of a timeless Creation if we know our place
and its gateway and ground is PEACE, as you proclaimed.

Come to the church at the bottom of the world
'through caverns measureless to man...'
where the sun of the world hangs, at midnight—
come back to the beginning: breathe, surrender, see.

CARDIFF ANGEL

On a single pillar beyond the museum
she stands above the fallen
their names carved in its totem of stone
profile silhouetted in the slowly fading light
winged plumage swept behind her
as if by a wind, cast in troubled silence—

and grasping something uprooted in her hand
with its small stick trunk and black roots dangling
and what is it ? The Tree of Peace ?
The Root of Civilization ? And is it
to be planted or torn apart ?
We can't answer. Only her face

serious as your questioning, and ours
mirrored by the question
and therefore standing, gazing, lingering.

Mewanwhile the tall old-fashioned lamps
illuminate around her like moons
and beyond, the copy-cat London Eye
still in its frozen white ferris wheel
for the Winter Wonderland that is to come.

Timeless, beautiful, defiant
she stands with her gesture and message
until peace returns
and woman stands as she is
I will hold this tree root in my hand
like a question unanswered, for the earth

as the sky deepens in the early dark, moving lights
and all the women in black with their bare flesh
as if at a funeral, echoing Saturday Night
with its shouts that are cries.

Psyche

DREAM QUATRAINS

1.

I will come and see you by troth.
The buttons of pearl are sewn onto his shirt.
Show me where the midnight fountain is.
I am lost in this dark forest of words.

2.

A fungus grows upon the brain.
Like a dark cap it runs with woodlice.
Under it we see the court jester's cap.
It is ringing with the bells of the morning.

3.

I know you love me beyond words.
You have placed in my hands the rose, the key.
It comes out of the depth of your body.
I have forsaken it with meaning.

4.

The night owl has come to silence us
Dawn steals in with its slowworm's song
Daylight lifts the axe to the trees
And the running blood-sap is full of gold and treasure.

HAIKU BLOSSOM I

White hail, lashing
White snowdrops, bowing
In the freezing wind...

Gospel of birdsong:
Sweetness after the suffering
Of freezing rain

They say: we sing after the pain,
After the rain comes the song

Here is the moment of clear sky
And calm:

Take it !

HAIKU BLOSSOM II

To sit still long enough
To hear a great wind outside
Circling our silence.

This is the other way
Into a world
That we rarely see or know.

We are too full of our faces
But now we breathe out of them—
In spite of ourselves, we let go.

A FREE ASSOCIATION IN THE NAME OF ANNA O.

For I am the whore and the holy one...
—'Thunder, Perfect Mind'

O Anna
you are a woman no one can help

Anna O
you lie there like an open wound
                              oozing symptoms

Anna original
without you we would have no vocation
no talking cure   no inquiry into compassion

No O, no Herr Professor Freud   no Doctor Bruer with his
bunch of roses   no countertransference in his eyes

You are the mother of our science

you unsung diva on your helpless couch of days and nights

And because you are a woman, wide open
you are every opening

Anna
            orifice   Anna anus   Anna ear nose & throat   Anna
orgasm

Anna the *materia* without which no
OOO no only

a phallocentric tower pointing up as useless as an abandoned
lighthouse
                  a lipstick peeling

and the suffering unseen river of the world below

with every daughter of the moon
wading unseen in its black waters

Narcissus there trying to fix his own reflection in a cracked hand
mirror he got Nth hand in a shop for the homeless

And Everyman wandering blind without a stick in a ceaseless
collision of ghosts   like tube doors closing

as they become a battlefield

as they become what we know only too well   and perpetuate

every ignorant dickhead who negates the soul

that lives in every woman's womb

O Anna
lamb of our prurient probings

Anna
madamoiselle of flirtatious excess (c/o Susannah York)

whore of our unknowing
                              the word made flesh

Anna
with your sex between two fingers
laughing as you lean back

holding the first and the last card
                              the Ace

of your latent liberation

AFTER RIMBAUD

*I ! I called myself a magician, an angel, free from all moral constraint.
...I am sent back to the soil to seek some obligation, to wrap gnarled
reality in my arms ! A peasant !*
—Season In Hell (1873) , trans. Paul Schmidt

Long long ago, a hundred thirty years at least
When you tramped the summer road to the Green Cabaret
Your life dust in the fields (dust that was on your boots)
You may even have reincarnated twice—
And yet you're twice as alive, being who you are
But who is that ? Is it you ? It's who we dream you as
That you dreamt yourself, writing hell in that hay barn,
Not that tanned silenced poet in the shadow of the sun
Or a man dying humiliated with a gangrenous stump
But of that magic you renounced we feed on as our own:
J'est un autre, you said, and it's true, we dream you other

Strange then to think of your life or mine
Become a dream long after we have gone—
A movie in anyone's eyes: was it ever our own ?

LANGUAGE, AT ANY MOMENT

for Tim Allen

1

Fieldfares exploding into the anticipation of the sky—
Breeze whispering through the ripening corn.

Blood red poppies. *It's not sex we deny, but death* you say
Blood red vermilion, alive

At my feet, the fallen feather of a hawk.

The area before the stile crowded with ox-eye daisies,
Their faces raised

The sky through my eyes speaking to them

2

Transparency is not just meaning
But matter infused with spirit—
A script every moment is unfolding.

Language without this is nothing
But more dead feathers—a victim's
(Scruffed grey and spat out down).

An overgrown path no one wants to seem to walk
Then the broad avenue of corn

Dividing these vast open fields

3

No ideas, but in things
And a thing without idea is a no-thing.

Ideas are like the wind
And they rest within, invisibly breathing.

4

If you cannot see matter as spirit
You can't see anything.

5

From corn gold to sand gold brown
A startled lark silently dipping and rising away

Then above the breeze
The first fragments of song.

And the sun.

BLUE

for Daisy Tufnell

But the jewel you lost was blue.
—Ted Hughes, *Birthday Letters (final line)*

1.

It's where you reach the end of the map.

Vast open sky as if eating into the ground
and yet the path is still here under your feet,
and the day is bright.

Where do you go, what do you do ?

Fear, that tells you
as it spins in your belly
that everything you know
has been outstripped—

Nothing is holding you.

And as quickly, it turns, reversing
(Nothing is holding you *back*)

And you turn, you spin
you dervish-dance with your arms outstretched
joyous, releasing and strengthening

in your newfound element

2.

Imagine: everything you know about yourself
become merely a part of something greater and unnamed
—*actress, poet, dancer, therapist, healer*—
as you surround yourself
in a deep blue cowl.

You dwarf yourself,
you become the sky standing over you
at this intersection of dimensions
in an aura that is still physically you.

Then you see the island again
the high promontory, the deep reach of sea

then in an instant, like a great ring flashing and connecting
you stand where far past and future meet
in the Being that has always been you

—*now.*

3.

Who do you think you are ?
It's this blue part that drives the car
that instructs you like an instrument
more fragile than glass

How tiny you are
how easily broken in your creaturely beauty

And because you don't know where you're going
you can have compassion for yourself
and humility.

There's not even the map you had—the air will not answer
or rather, its brightening blue *is* the answer

And what do you do when you don't even know that?
You wait for a signpost, like a sight test
through the emptiness

4.

And what do you have here?
What do you hold in your hands?
(What rested on the back of yours,
and on your binding ring...)

One imperative, that is breathing
that is your heart's fire—
and your body's moving

The only thing you have, having nothing
as it spells itself out: C R E A T E
an acrostic scored in cloud-foam...

any way you read it, back to front and upside down.

5.

'You're bigger than the stars, so you watch them dance'
you say with a cryptic smile
as you sit cross-legged on your floor

There are no rules here—and yet there are
when we enter the presence that is now
in each cell of our body

And if the mirror of the air can stay clear
we know what is right that's true for both of us
as it breathes and lingers in the space between...

And what's right one moment can be wrong the next,
we will never take it for granted again
every moment in the garden is new as it is fresh
it's only you in your grey mind that can't see it
stumbling stupidly over the flower beds

And what's true here is always true
Blue means 'out of the blue', when you least expect it—

The shock of being who you are at any moment
that finds you here alive.

SELF-PORTRAIT

after the painting by Zdislaw Ruszkowski (c. 1967)

This is Modern Man:
diseased in the place of vision
his brow as if bared to the brain
—a whited cauliflower, with its stem
extending like a handle to the end of his nose...

Green about the gills, from the jacket to the neck
lime green like a grass stain, cheap green like disco light
and the face with its ambiguous pencilled moustache
and great open sad eyes, half in shadow
(hairline above receding into white)
that say it all: not mean at heart
only bemused by all he has seen
across a century of catastrophe—

and with the whole of his forehead
as if crying out for a hand of light

even as the sun seems to be brightening
from his own (is it ? Could it be ?)
invisible attending Self—
his spirit-level sight.

PSI-LOGIC

Smoke rising vigorously
in a vertical column from no.3
dark grey into the January twilight—
and the off-white of the cloud massed above

lifting a man's heart into home fires that were,
a hundred years ago or more, or just in childhood,
timeless and rare past this millenium...

But then he realizes why he's staring
as another plume of smoke rises
sickeningly skywards, reminding him
outside the walls of that North Italian town
as he hovers, all disembodied eye now,
suddenly caught by surprise
his whole mind become a cinema
flooded with awe and grief—
watching his former laboratory
razed to the sky.

He looks up at his own house now
two doors along, at the compact white tower of it,
and at the windows he's left open
to let out a different smoke...

the acrid stench of sage and lavender
soaked with the psyche's pleading
and all the laundry of the mind
to give him a clear space to be

closer to that ever-present
unreachable ancient future blue,
realer than real behind this screen.

ANGEL OF THE INNER EAR

from an anonymous channelled painting

Thin as a surgical bone needle, and as sharp
eyes the size of tiny antennae ends
hair a flaring mohican of light
diaphanous wings raised in an aureole of colour,
radiating up and out in its climbing arc
of blue green and red gold

suddenly become what it is: an ear !
In its flame-shape set against the velvet darkness,
an ear vibrating with clairaudient sound

And this angel at its centre,
defying all our conceiving—

that something so vast could also be so small
shrunk into a faery butterfly
with a hole in her chest where her heart is streaming
squeezed into absolute service, selfless

in the chamber of your hearing
transmitting each note she embodies,
hovering, out of her finest nectar...

knowing the glory is her Creator's
and in the hand of the artist who drew this
as it flashed into her inner seeing, complete

from the soul of sound, that can be
synapses firing in a circuitboard, circumscribed;
and something ever more miraculous
we can still only barely imagine:

a world within a world where we have our being
a world of light, closer than our breath—
counting every hair on your head.

YOU

for the daimon, and the angel

So there are two of us,
there always have been—
in every moment of seeing or understanding,
in every gesture of finer love
where I thought there was *I* there was *you*
my mirror, and yet not me or mine—*you*, other
and we are together for as long as I am here
where I go, you follow, wherever I go
inside the being of my skin
my innermost being that is *you*

So when I die, who will remain ?
Is it you who swims through the dissolving air
to the tunnel's end, and stands in the light ?
You, my truest and highest ?
Or do you carry me, like I do my beloved tomcat
home like a lamb to the fold ?
Then who am I ?
                    At last I hear you say

All I am is also you,
all we are is what breathes through me
being what we do...
when you truly come to give,
you will understand this.

There is a memory of who we've been in life,
and as you are what is inside you
I am what is inside me
and he is returning veil by veil, as you are
clothed here in flesh, in the cloak of your skin;

and when we die there there is only the light
the heart's dream of all we have been
that we long to help you to be...

All we are in our innermost hearts, like a star,
that is as He was in the beginning—
a primal spark of love

                        in the womb-heart of silence.

SONGTHRUSH

outside Shelley's Hotel, Lynmouth

First glimpsed in the twilight
as your exuberant song fills the air
where we can't see you or what you are
perched high in the bare twigs of a buddleia
in front of a house's vertical white facade

sheathed in twilight, blackbird-sized
or lark, but neither—
and louder than anything else in town !
Natural jazzman and crooner,
your five minute solos punctured by pauses

before your next routine begins...
In the morning light now, nearer the ground,
with the old slate church roof behind you
your speckled throat, glorious
your song as mischevious

stalling six walkers for an audience
and in the royal cause of birdsong.
Later you sing the whole of the churchfront
with its rising grey and red granite
and silent bells that ring out...

cocking your head again, listening for worms.
Improviser, mimic and innovator
one minute, commanding
the next, cajoling
then shrieking like an oyster catcher—

before something entirely new breaks in
unrehearsed, uncovered, a jewel of phrasing
in the sweet river of your imagining

a trilling somersault, a soft low note fading
before your standards re-enter

Listen now ! Come on, keep going !
you seem to say—play on, sing on
in spite of everything, and the dross
as the gold light illuminates you
and the morning finds you again

at your post, accomplishing your task
to stop the world until it harkens again
to you, dear bird of earth,
and to the wind and sea beyond
the seagulls wheeling, and the music of the spheres

and the world may listen then
as we are listening now.

ANTONIA

1.

Tales of pain and indecision
a racked crossing, either way, of an invisible bridge
as the tide came and went
and then, at some point, no way back.

Something is seeded in the body
that is not only the body
that makes it blossom
manly or womanly—or somewhere between,
and 'somewhere between' in all of us
in our liminal duality, liquid as the tide,
and your two fish swimming oppositely, side by side.

A man that was a woman,
a woman who was a man.
A man who wants to be a woman,
a man who is also a woman

deep down
in the truest invisible part of him,
rising like the stem of an impossible flower.

Only a dusting of fine hair on the lip
short brown hair turned blown-dry blonde;
her greeting a determined kiss on the mouth
her nervous hospitality as fulsome
as cleavage where there was none,
bulging softly under stretched grey.

Stretched as we are...and as I sit between you
on the big broad salmon pink sofa
in our tennis match of rapid, just-arrived conversation
turning my head one way, then the other—

seeing you, with your raised cavalier face
pronounced nose and cheekbones
looking as masculine as 'she' looks feminine:
so, are we all in disguise ?

And you become two souls, once husband and wife
your roles discarded like clothes...although
your son is also somewhere in this dream house,
trying to find his way between tide and shoreline,
where our minds make and break their contours
in an eternal, ever-deepening sea.

2.

A rack of transitional garments
short-sleeved shirts, and skirts beneath
in sequined deep-water glitter
the tide outside rippling in
candescent in the soft grey island light.

Venus born from the waves,
androgynous in the shell of time.

And on the attic landing, your face there
in a starched shirt and dark-lined suit,
hair backcombed and brylcreemed
slightly protruding ears and sensual lips
the expression unmistakeably you
in the woman within you rising
questioning even then, or knowing
this is who I am, not what you've made of me.

3.

'It's when you get up in the morning
and look in the mirror' ,you're saying,
'how comfortable are you with what you're seeing ?'
—knickers pegged out on a washing line
above the road where we're driving—
And then imagine standing there and feeling
this is not who I need to be, seeing
a woman inside a man, built of eyes
of soul-light, meeting you...

And to see her always as your other, calling you
like Eurydice, to turn and embrace her
to finally have to be her ?

And the reality of surgery, to see
his/her face reduced to a bleeding pulp
for his to become hers...the jaw scraped,
forehead lifted, cheeks raised like the voice
in its larynx perched to a quavering
unmistakeable height
vulnerable to your irritation
at being mimicked
by what seems inauthentic, crying out
from a truth so deep and so painful
the pain of torn skin can barely match it
but strangely as relief, as proof of it...

We drive on the island-bisecting road, in silence.

4.

Eating Danish pastries in the breeze-blown garden
as you sit side by side in a one-piece bench
with its two seats angled towards each other,
bare feet tucked up, painted toenails visible,

as we talk about the novels stacked inside your house,
which are worth reading, and what it means
to need to express oneself in an object
external to ourselves as evidence
that a greater part of us exists—

And you need no proof: all I have, you have
from inside your own body, and as you say
(without meaning to in any way offend)
'To listen to one thrush is worth a thousand poems'

And where you run in the Sunday morning breeze,
the poem is you: your true life, or nothing
being far more alive than you ever were
so what else do you need ? Not art, but a mirror
reflecting eyes of love, of longed-for understanding.

5.

The key to the doorless gap in the wall opened
by a mother duck with her wingflash of blue
standing guard with her brood of chicks
bee-brown and fluffy by the enclosed pond's edge...

And the holy well garden is empty for us,
for these brief moments in the sun
with its uneven slant of upwards ground
sloping to its miniature cliff-edge
as you sit in the high corner beside the iron ladder stile

Eyes closed in the breeze, with the clouds
bright against the blue, airbrushed cirrus,
the need for sanctuary as timeless
as St. Seriol himself here, and in all of us
who have fed peace to this place
from inside ourselves, and received it.

Something as clear as this square of water
laced with shells and glittering new bronze coins
catching the light like windows blazing
and unruffled, crystal, simple
to sit here and be as still
knowing who you are in the eye of God
for no other reason, but because
your heart tells you it is so.

Anglesey

BLACK SHUCK

for Janet Bord

Coal-black apparition, blocking our climb
electric with shadow, who are you ?
When you will not move in the still air
where we can hear our breathing—
you will neither bark nor swing your tail
and there are no pools where you had eyes

Who are you? Death, or a warning
to the right path where this hazy path divides ?
We cannot say. In the haunting that fills the wood
that is your element, peeled back from underneath
all thought and sound, the truth that is unspeakable;
only visible, like everything that determines our way.

Blackstable Woods, Longridge, Painswick Valley, Glos.

from MIDNIGHT SUN

1. *after a metal relief by Maxine Relton*

Dusky gold on mountains
mirrored in their view
bathed in moonlight—

You have come to the final passage of night.

To close your eyes and find yourself
in a heaven of mountains
all made of a lava-flow of gold.

And depth and height are one,
and depth and height were one.

Tell us the name of these mountains,
they are the Midnight Sun.

And walking on air, on cloud
and walking on ground are

one dream of the sun.

The other is being one
with everything you see now,
all senses tuned to luminous night

when even the tip of your tongue turns to gold
your radiant smile not of this world

but of a world you've always known.

5.

Do you remember ? The glassy pond
behind the old mill house with its stream
there among the fields, in a cleft
between rising bank and fence...

It had been raining as we walked
then as we climbed to its edge
looking among the overhanging trees
to where the little boat is moored

the sun came out, as the raindrops
began to drip from the branches
onto the meniscus of the water
and as they fall, sparkling

catching fire with the light !
each one flaring, firefly-like
then its bubble bursting—
as soon as seen, gone...and we

held our breath standing there
in the beauty of it, and the light
that shone back through the gunnera
veined, transparent, touched you too

as the raindrops went on falling, igniting

and the light that made us ache
to see it, in its blazing truth

pressed up against our hearts for an answer.

8.

The sun's dark horses call your heart away
—Richard Burns, *'For George Seferis II'*

Because, deep down
you don't feel worthy
you turn away from love

because you fear
being hurt again
you keep your heart on ice

despite your smile, your laughter, even.

All you have left is your freedom
from everything, and the world.
So you live in poverty.

The sun' s dark horses
circle your horizon.

All you have left is your sex
so you give it to a man who can't meet you

All you have left is your voice
so you sing like a woman burning

Finally, there's nowhere to hide.
It is time to face the sun

your heart (at last) calling the tune.

10.

for H.S.

Your first awakening, more precious than anything
(as the whole of this streetside cafe disappears
like candlelight for a moment behind your eyes)
that 'Henry' was a complete invention
he'd never existed, and never would—
plunging you into Being, and the witness...

Only to find, second time
that the witness doesn't exist either !
bouncing you back off the wall of death
into all this is, which is totally Here Now
you and I talking, as our light intensifies
sparking from phrase to phrase, in instant
recognition and laughter, of its own making
(essence to essence and human, purely soul
I would say, with all the words I have left)

And your brown-black eyes still beckoning
towards the nothing that liberates everything
the koan at the centre of the turning world
that is the bridge that crossses the river
where the bridge is moving and the river is still
stopping your mind until the understanding comes
as it did before, with the sound of one hand
bubbling up like laughter from your depths

releasing our bellies briefly into quivering joy
that is the light we know in everything.

17.

Come back to the true path of gold
beyond all that your body knows
and all that your feelings have felt
in the dark where the sun has gone down

and the night is drowning. Wake up now
the light is calling you in its silence
its bird-sung serenity, invisibly smiling,
to pour through you and lift all weight away;

all anxiety of self that separates you
all illusion of loneliness, until you know
the vastness you are part of you can choose
or deny, veiled as it is for your own sake

so you can imprint your own soul's making
where everything is for our redeeming
and the only judgement is you—
like the only love that surrounds you

in all your surrender and becoming.

20.

You called me a Pharisee
so then why, when I reached out,
did you refuse the Christ in me ?

If I am your shadow, and you are mine,
then let's speak until we see each other's hearts
or we both hang from the Judas Tree.

25.

The question
why we suffer
what we do,
perhaps the only question

We are all
cracked open
from the stars
before we can find
what we came here to live

in our heart of hearts

or we'd remain
(as some of us strangely do)
schizoid, aloof
and with such pain

such pain refused
like permafrost
frozen with rage
it takes a flame-torch

to get through:
Isaac Newton, and you.

32.

Queen of the midnight sun
Mary, mother, veiled
palms raised open—
aureole surrounded by golden stars !

(above the shadow of an unlit candle)

and at the centre of her ruby red
clothed belly

in the archway of her gilt iconic frame

her vast darkness like an apron
falling away

and this blazing radiant child
brighter than a thousand suns
this baby that is for the world, you say,
and forever

standing naked
white transparent
gold as only gold can be
heated to its fineness

inviting you into
the child you were and are
in the light we were together in
the light that came before everything

*so complete we didn't even
need our names.*

36.

Inner beauty, inner truth
breathing in silence inside the body
alive in each cell
each heartbeat of feeling, longing
grieving, awakening
and in each unspoken thought

that drops like a stone
deep into a well—
as we sit to write, huddled
in this silent cottage
under its low-beamed ceiling,
in the still midwinter
of our midnight world.

A stone in clear water,
splash-rippling and sinking
in and out of
our innermost being...

that says: *wordless indelible
presence knows all—
future poetry—pure experience's door.*

38.

Your gift to know
in precious, invisible gold
blackened in your mystery

that all a heart can feel
in love and its opposite
is part of me

and its gift to you, now
the deepest love that is
the deepest dark, too—

(that has been there
and is pledged to go on
harrowing its own hell)

in no longer trying
to be pure and removed
you have found the elusive Stone

and its secret: *in meeting*
all that is shadow in our own heart
it can transform—

and in all your listening
pausing and reflecting
you know what rings true: one for all.

from ANAMNESIS

written as poet in residence at St. James' Church, Piccadilly
for my mother Yvonne (1915-1976) & father Donald (1917-2007)
Anne Jorgensen, and Martin Palmer

1.

Traveller: stop a moment.
It is time to stop time, to step inside.
Come into this house of quiet
and let it take your mind. Can you ?
The hardest thing. To stop thinking.
So you can start really seeing
and enter the silent mind
that waits in the stillness, and your breathing.

Can you sit still ? Can you let
everything be around you?
Then you will find new eyes
and the rose in your heart will open.
Then you will know what is true
infinitely made for you, in each moment;
this dew drop, this day's pearl
this grit irritating deep in your being
where everything is reflected to you.

Traveller, who are you? Under your name
your occupation and your clothes
you are formless consciousness living in time
with a strange disposition to love.
Dear naked soul, come home.

3.

What is the gift of your life ?

Beyond naming, an utterance
in your throat's depth, your soul's
intention to live—

Can you recall it ?
You sit in meditation, surrounded by stars.

What are you living for ?
There is an answer so personal
so passionate, beyond all conceiving
in your innermost coding—
that your secret may die with you,
but not before you've had the chance
to witness its luminous traces.

And she, he is your answer
that other one nearest of all within
who shines in you like an icon, a sun.

What else is there ? The spiral climb
hearing your name called through the mist,
ever-stretched towards your blue potential
true self's surrender, that is the only way home.

4.

Do you remember what we did
in those desperate times
when we met?

I would scratch a small circle in the dust
and you would add another, overlapping
and in that simple ritual moment
heaven and earth were reconciled again.

It's a secret we seem to have forgotten:
one thing alone can never be the truth,
it takes two—it takes opposition—
but only when two are brought together
and blended, can there be resolution
at the unforeseen higher, holy place.

Sacred sex, and union between nations
tortured by being held apart
in the agony of fundamental righteousness.
While, as only God knows,
when I surrender to you, as you do to me
even a little, then true light returns—
born out if its shadow, glimmering, gold.

7.

It's like a wave—a hundred faces
lying, stooping, standing or sitting
stretched from end to end of the canvas
all of us in the middle of an ordinary day
brooding, gazing, dreaming, grieving

that means we are together and alone
in the community we live in
that is *village*—which also means
we are beyond each other's choosing...

Can we believe that everyone we find
is meant to be a thread in our lives
part as we all are of each other ?

That there are no real strangers
only strangely familiar faces
repeated across time, witnessing
that we are closer to each other than we know ?

But only if we take care, great care
of each other as we may learn to of ourselves
like a second skin, but of one flesh beneath—

that is the truth we hardly dare recognize
mixing morality and offal; love, and raw exploding meat.

8.

So what do we listen to
the greater love or the the greater fear ?

How can we find
each other as we are ?
The enemy within
is also of our choosing.

He may even strike you with a smile,
or you imagine her eyes are cold.

Only the centre that cannot be breached
is the centre that can hold.

And that means holding it, too
so that the white circle of our sanctuary
is clear—where we can confuse
love with the realm of its living,
losing the ground of our union.

But still, when we return to it
we may find each other again
in an ever-deepening warmth beyond all reason
more than ready to forgive us.

Lord, help us to return to each other
into the only community there is—
transcending our separate skins.

9.

What does it really mean
to be free in your body ?

To stand authentically,
to move, only moved from within
to let the music be you.

It's like true love—discovered,
rising in bubbles of cells
like blood, electric
with their own purpose
from their all seeing sense...
in the darkness of transparent flesh.

For every gesture we make
to be from this within
is at last to stand on hallowed ground

in the fine gravity of all we can utter
in a language that transcends our origin

becoming the Word that was the beginning
when all we are was breathed into being;

only now, we may live to see it.

13.

Pure womb of sound:
gold struck to its depth
resonant, echoing,
out of each hammered bowl;
and with a gentleness
that is beyond this world
yet as deeply scored within it...

dancing over the river of blood
like gnats in the evening light
the sweet gold water whispering

its wave-sounds rippling
tender as breath inside the body;
each lingering echo a remembering
soothing the ear to its song
it is always quickening...

and as the windchimes swing
outside in the sanctuary garden
through the London darkness

Sound
becoming Word
for what was Paradise
and is, in every living cell
when the peace of heaven
re-enters us at will—

And then, as now, all shall be well
all manner of things shall be themselves
in every language in the world.

14.

The circle makers have come.
Have no doubt
about the mysterious white lights
high vibrating sounds, swirling air,
and the amazement you feel or fear
at what you see, scrolling
across the pages of the open fields...

It is all intended.
From star-seed to Gaia
in the one star body we are
being part of
one forgotten language
of symbolic cosmic energy
re-awakening and aligning us.

Raise your eyes,
raise your dead perceptions
we are stardust in our robes of skin
on a journey of incarnation and return
and the hand they reach out for us
the continual hand, that defies all triviality
in a rage of beauty and clarity
is our future, if we want it

where we'll never stop creating
under the Ancient Sign

held by the deepest archetypes of life
among these hieroglyphics of the True Divine.

16.

'Do this', he said
'in memory of me'
All it is, and all it's been

to remember who you
really are within
that he gave his life for
and his name

that is our name too
from the stars: *Christos*

And gave it as no one had
with a love that had never been
which is still about to be

Do this in memory of me

All I am and all I have
is yours, that passionate surrender
for all lovers, for all time
and a bright inexplicable ghost
transubstantiating anywhere

that is our resurrection
still saying what is ours to say
and be, in all our centres: *I am here.*

A DREAM FOR EASTER

Leonardo saw it first:
in this copy of his painting
archetypal as a Tarot card, but living
in the library of a great house
where all the shelves are empty

And you, mysterious Christ, are standing
in a trailing bridal veil—
but gold-pleated, reaching in front of you
wound round your crucified body like a memory

And your lips are sealed, veiled
covered in a *burqa* of thin white muslin
in this secret of your ressurrecting
that every man needs to hear
glowing all around you like lamplight...

And you are the female face of a man
who does nothing but speak
until the woman beside him is screaming;
you are the third body of healing between them

as the dream voice says you are *icthys*—fish
a man and a woman fish that is
the whole we never dreamt we could dream.

INSIDE THE WIND

1.

Where I come from in this stillness is the infinite sun.

You know where I come from in this softness and peace between us is the infinite sun.

I have no name but where our names are one—I am Beloved known by a name that denies my singular origin.

My name means I am Beloved of God. I am loved in the sun.

How can we not be in communion with all there is ?

The light shines through us continually streaming through everything.

It is our life and Source, visible and invisible.

But we can pretend it isn't, and live in denial of each other.

We can pretend—and for so long we believe the lie.

We are liars in the light, with the sun on our faces.

And the light never leaves us. It simply shines on.

And whatever we do with our lives, the vast community of the dead awaits us—

the people of the infinite sun.

2.

Wind. The wind outside this London evening restless among the chimes and howling at the edges of the house. You can't keep the wind out. It's like the air you breathe, only stronger. Look ! It even opens the heavy black front door wide that you left unlocked for our late guest. And the wind is that guest. The Second Coming that is air.

3.

Even the chorus of sirens that race down the wind-filled tree-lined avenue become one extending, flanked, echoic, billowing music.

UNICORN

You're waiting below—you're ready,
it's me that's late. Bareback, white-grey
goat-grounded, but unmistakeable
with your spiralling horn and forelock.
Unicorn.

The realest you can be
here in this sandy woodland—and attuned
to the slightest twitch of invisible reins
or my boot, to accelerate away
faster than any motorbike
fast as sound and the speed of light—
to where the air is white heat all around us
and we're flying...

Unicorn: to be that free
to say what only I can, that is you
within: being so much more than I can be
you at my fullest and finest
and least fearing—as hard to believe

Your gift you drop, dog-like, in front of my feet
a half chewed cud like a brick
I wonder at: *nourishment*
for the earth that feeds you
that gives you your superdrive

from the deepest earth to the highest light
embodied, magnified...

Not tall in hands, but as long
as I could stretch out to lie on
and sometimes let you take me there;

but then to wake and be that rider
who is duty-bound to the dawn.

DESTINATION UNKNOWN

after seeing White Unknown Male, C4, Dec.'06

White space, whited-out mind. Imagine
waking up and finding
that you can't remember anything
about who or where you are—
all the tall buildings outside the train strange
as its unknown destination

You have arrived
at the Coney Island of the Mind
and for real, in a hospital of agonies
where yours is that you are no one
with nothing but an A to Z of New York
with its pink slip of paper, and the name
of a woman who barely remembers you either.

No one's even sure you're telling the truth—
it's so unbelievable, after all
to be wandering around so naked
neither drunk, stoned or psychotic
—no episode at all—but as stripped
as the day your spirit was born

and as conscious too, as your adult eyes
(all language and motor skills intact)
staring into the whirling circus of life
but from inside the wheel, transparently
simple and immediate—and in your joy
standing in the sea as the waves break in
pure energy streaming into your skin...

Who are you now ? Who are we ?
Jesus without a family, our children
not our children (as Gibran advised)

your father's face as perplexed
not knowing how to answer you...

And what are all these things we accumulate
in our fragile memory-bound identity
in a store room in Paris without their owner
but a 'bizarre bricolage', as you phrase it
tired Green Room props ready for charity
but not who we are, as you begin to see it

walking free (still supported on either side)
imagine being that light and you will find
the one in you who can't be put down
to names, places or possessions
but who is always breathing and being
through the human experience we're having
here, and at one remove (as He was)
in the Self that is your nameless name.

Love has found you too, in this dream
in a new spring, in a London park, walking
with a woman who can see you as you are.
'No future, no past'. What the Indians meant
by being alive as we are, and brave
warriors for life (as for love, now)
polite at the bar as you join in
with your old English cronies, leaving them
wondering who the hell *they* are...

What greater gift ? Everywhere you go
only to know from the unnameable
that who we are is visibly invisible:
more a mystery than we've ever been
and more ourselves, in reality.

THE PALACE OF GOD

at Gaunts House, Wimborne, Dorset

In a little marquee on his own
with the festival milling all around him
a Tibetan monk is making a mandala in sand.

Laid out to the four directions—
an amazing candy palace, filling our eyes
edible like some fabulous communion wafer
colours like candy, childhood sweets, innocence.
He smiles wordlessly. Pink, yellow, lime green
light blue and mauve...every inch a formal garden
entrances, arches, squares within squares
bells in each of its corners—a vision
of unbelievable precision.

His English-speaking frontman friend hovers
willing to translate, as we gaze on
I ask how does it feel to do this ?
Like building the Palace of God, the answer comes
silencing our incomprehension
with another smile, like happiness.
What else is there to do ? And in two days
it will no longer exist, surrendered to transience;
The Palace perpetually unfixed.

His friend explains the surrendering
cause and effect, right action and karma
but I'm watching his finger smoothing the edge
to a hairsbreadth among the sandgrains
as the knot in my stomach clenches.
To build the Palace of God without fear
poet of sand, with all we can build with
letting our works go; and anyway knowing
that in two days all this will change
fear and love will pass away:

to build itself enough, being happiness.

Ways of Love

A KEEPSAKE

Tableau: they stand through the window
Just the other side of our conversation
With the ice cream remains on the table
As she reaches up to where the roses climb above them
—pink and white in full abundant blossom—
Baring her pregnant stomach, as her blouse lifts:
'Smell them', she says to him, and as she stretches
Rose petals rain down like confetti, they touch her skin,
As he obliges—willing as he has been

And she is ? 17, and he is, more or less
About to be parents with no more clue
Than we have about what will be
As we sit on this unspoken edge of our fears—
Only, what it is that holds them invisibly
As we do our breath—and who knows, maybe the less
We know, the more we can feel, in the trust it takes
To reach for those roses and be showered in beauty ?

I will keep your image before me.

AFTER RUMI

for S.

Of course we tell each other everything,
That's what lovers are supposed to do.

Can we make a blossoming
With only one pair of hands ?

The pearl we are has to be cracked open,
Before it becomes a pearl.

Don't fear your mouth
There's nothing to lose,
Only the cage of your unspeaking...

These words you are brought to
Are another kind of river—

The sweet water that wants
To flow through you like fire.

AFTER RUMI II

When he gets to the other side
He dances a song of ecstasy and praise with his whole body !

He can't believe what he sees—
The whole universe turned inside out from the heart all around
him !

He flings his arms open wide—
Releasing the chains from inside each cell of him...

And do we have to wait till we die ?
Will that be our greatest regret ?
That we never knew *life* ?

Back here, we grow older in boxes
Psychologically aware, in our stylish boxes

While what he says is
If you haven't learnt to praise and dance
The whole of your inner being stays closed like a door—

And you might as well have learnt nothing at all.

AFTER RUMI V

Occluded sun—
Over the misty rain hills

This is Your Light
Like a candle in the depths

Saying *the clouds of the visible world*
Are our own—

And the ones we need
To find each other

And You within us
Where no sun shines

As what we know
Rises in our blood

Mirrored
In every act of love

Part of the Greater World
We cannot see:

Strange, to have eyes—
Yet to have none.

AFTER RUMI VIII

Why is it we can only love
What is unavailable ?

Are we really so terrified
Of the real thing ?

She wanders the late streets.

She has fantasies of being
Impregnated by the guru.

And I want to say to her
Love, I'm here—are you ?

I want to gently
Shake her out of her daze

I want to say
It's *all* of us, anywhere now

Is it only when the guru dies
That we can truly inhabit ourselves,
Knowing what we know, from the sun ?

Rumi smiles as if to say
That's why I never set up as one

But: love is not love
Until it's been to the grave.

AFTER RUMI IX

You can say what you like—
It isn't necessarily what you feel

You can name what you aspire to,
But it isn't what you practise.

Language is an elephant,
An emperor, a hollow reed...

Find the words that are your own
Fired from inside your skin

And from the place where you had nothing
But broken husks and shells of meaning

Then when you speak
You will say what you mean.

BY SNOWSHILL STREAM

for Susie

Strands of her blond hair floating in the dream,
Falling suddenly, shockingly, dry on wet—
All of its long Swedish length he sheared for her
Chosen purification, into the water...years ago, gone now

Even as its impact remains, as I imagined it, told
And have done since—in fact every time I've stood on this
bridge;
Exquisitely arched in its Cotswold stone, two paces long...
Invisibly now as the water's meniscus in the evening light
Now so many other feet have been here, other eyes
And thoughts, building these child-like dams
The water layers itself down over

As you swing silently behind me
On the white makeshift seat with its struts of blue rope
Hanging from the alder's generous branch,
Resting in your silence, as I squat on dried cow-mud, seeing

That as deep as we may see
The earth remembers nothing but its own secrets
That are as invisible to us—
The earth only remembers its life
In a maze of rootlets, tendrils and sliding
Scurrying, burrowing creatures—

And us ? Playing as we are, always seriously,
Whatever our size and age—and as fleetingly
Maybe the earth remembers a little of what it chooses to
In the graced veils of her places, which have been graced,
By loving eyes or sacrifice, something worth dreaming...

Or as our eyes meet silently—
The way you might remember me.

BEING YOU

for P.

Can it be done ?

Imagining a day in your life
(sitting under this oak
with its broad view down...)
I can finally step beyond myself
finally ? No, remarkably soon

as open as I am
                        or can let myself be

like now, as you fill my eyes—
and all the landscape is what you're seeing
as close as I begin to feel your breathing
as you pause, in your particular concentration...

then you are inside me, as you begin to speak
and your words cross the page inside my own
like a letter you're writing in my skin

and the you that is inside me
for this brief time
    like a visitation
        from beyond this plane

is blessedly more
                        than the me

ECSTASIS

Launched, yearning, ecstatic, blending—
and then the gap

where we're left outside of ourselves
as if locked out of our house—

This is the shadow side, the dark moon of love.

We've wandered over this London Hill in the twilight
as its island of grass surrounds us like a sea
almost agoraphobic, as I squat down

in this strange sickening between us.

This is the borderland, the danger zone
where we can linger like the souls of the dead
until we find the way back.

What way ?

Finally I see it as I see your face
(helpless and frustrated as you also feel)
—then I'm free.

I don't have to disengage, or play the game
all I have to do is tickle back
my soul into my body like a trout

then I can love you in spite of everything
and breathe.

GETTING THROUGH

'Will you hold me now ?', she says, her eyes shut,
reaching out her hands blindly—
as if suddenly eleven years old again...

and a man three thousand miles away in South Carolina
just out of the shower, tidying his holiday apartment,
picks up a lock of her hair stashed in an envelope
wondering if she and it are still alive to him

and closing his eyes, as the current he knows surges,
finds himself saying 'Yes—I will'.

MONTSEGUR

I can see it all—
The high cobbled streets leading to where you're speaking
With the valleys below you over the edge...
The water faucet dripping its bright trail back down
Like a woman peeing

With the castle high on its crag above you, an hour's walk on.
'There are roses *everywhere*', you're saying
I can smell their light, as you talk on
And there was the blue butterfly that rested on your hand !
That brings the sky all round my ears, through you

Blue meaning you have come through to your own choosing
As it breathes between us in this unpolluted air

And there is a story we all share
In the terrible kiln of that castle yard
Burnt, escaping, or weeping secret tears
That we are still living now   regathered again

In a love that goes beyond all bounds
A dangerous love, that will not fit the rules
That shames the unbelievers with their unbelief
As it burns us to live it...
                              until we know

That plunging in its free-fall in the blue of it
Eagle-wise, crazy-wise, laughing-wise

Where vertigo becomes flight,
                              is the only way we can see

Between the binding that chains us,
and the Heart that holds us all.

THE BRIDGET CROSS

for B.

Four scissor-sharp slivvers of sapphire sky
centred into the saving sign—
where the leading thickens under your shaping fingers:

and still they pull apart in meeting
adjacent, asymmetrical—
miraculously crossed like jet trails
and like arms, eager to dance

And isn't this the Cross of Resurrection ?
A woman's cross, too, that is lightning
stained glass blue as the highest—
and the flash you know at the centre of your forehead
that guides you where you need to go...

With Him (our Master) free of all bondage
not nailed down to anything now—
free to love, storm-potent, and as still
as his eyes' unbroken gaze across the bridge of time.

from SOULMATE

3.

Your clear warm voice cuts through everything
—every complexity, every hesitation—
arriving at the thing itself in the first syllable
that so fits in my inner ear, nestling like a receiver
I don't even have to tilt my neck to hold

It isn't even a telephone—it's a whole world
opening its rose window from my heart
that becomes everything I'm seeing
gently taking its truest place
—these cars on the motorway, this destination—
to arrive where that other one inside us
knows we should be.

4.

And inside this, you are that ruby
—a locket of secret fire closed inward—
invisible in all the veins of my bloodstream,
where all we've felt that can blaze or radiate out
becomes in-folded into itself, in silence
(and is this is how we come to live in one another
not as form or face, but essence ?)

and I think this must be what makes a gem stone, and does:
fire reversed in the earth heart's core, cooling
in air that is water...hidden like a vein of gold
out of sight or mind—but impossible not to feel
as it rises anywhere, from underneath everything.

6.

The widest possible horizon
the globe like the sky between our eyes
and our minds—

and heart-to-heart and mind, in a connecting
that has no binding—
this rose-coloured elastic ease

like a harness for jumping into the void—
that can dance even when it's still,
and does.

You know what it means:
and freedom like this is vertiginous
taking us beyond our own fear of it,

in an anaesthesia of joy !

8.

Be still and know
that you are you

and all there is
is around you—

being you, come
to seek and find

in any and every moment

your Self,
the story of your life.

WRITING IN THE SAME ROOM

for Joanne, at Hawkwood

Brown flows into brown—
the stripped floor, the patterned carpet
congealing white

Lowered eyelids, the flickering hub of the candle
on the round glass table, glowing like a pumpkin

Neither of us looking, both plunged deep within
sculpted into the stillness of our postures...

Only after a while we notice without eyes
as one stops writing, and the other pauses
as our hands rest briefly

we surface like shy fish daring a glance
before returning under the skin

And there is a slow sun that rises without our knowing
that brings us both towards resolution...
in this quiet *coniunctio* breathing between us
that allows us to be alone together
and as intimate as anyone could be
after hours of conversation or sex
strangers as we are, beyond friends

Because I know you saw the same fox
ripped in half by the same careless driver
flattened there with his unmarked face and ears
catching in your throat and eyes, as it did mine
leaving us with the same wrenched question
that pulls us inside the entrails of our own being
to answer all we are here to live for

on the border where shadow meets light.

THE CONTRACT

for A.

We had a contract.
What does it mean ? What did it say—
when it is anything but words on paper

and yet as decided: binding even
(freely chosen as it had to be)
and what it looks like is

your face
lying beside me as our eyes meet
knowing without knowing we know
and not in ourselves, but in something
more deeply alive, more strangely certain

We would have said *our soules*

So that I can say to you, *yes, you can*
repeating it, without knowing what I mean
only knowing I mean it

and you can receive it, opening
the exquisite venus of your sex
to let it more deeply in
along all your silken underground walls

opening your throat, too
as you lean backwards into the sky of your cry

It's not a conceit this time—

And now we're lying here, inches apart
who are you ? Cathar, courtier, courtesan
'smack in the eye' you say, smiling
and how was it then ?

Were we both men
or—if you compass can stretch—
was I a woman, too ?

All we know is this moment of eyes
gazing evenly beyond time

All we know is we agreed to this
signed in secret fire
without need of further witness

releasing now, beneath them
in our hearts, our hands, in every vein

into this every day dawning that is
all that love can ever dream
My God, I have found you again.

THE STILLNESS

He cam also stille
Ther his moder was
As dew in Aprille
That falleth on the grass
—Anon, 15th C.

...then we lay down
side by side, to rest
and chest to chest
pressed singly together—

as Mozart's Requiem played
soothing our minds
breath by breath
into a living sleep

until the stillness came
like dew, and like fire
the stillness came between us
and made us one heart—

your eyes at last opening
your cheeks gently flushed
as we smiled everything
that could be said, instead

and you are not my mother
in the space she leaves you
as she smiles above us,
which means we can both be
truly blessed...

Anon, 21st C.

THE FOUNDATION

I have arrived at the foundation
and you are here to welcome me
queen of my heart, as you speak your truth:
'It doesn't matter what people say
it only matters what they do'.

ANSAPHONE MESSAGE

I'm just ringing because of what we're missing,
to reach out a hand to you. I don't need
to say anything to you,
and I don't want to get caught
in the sticky spider's thread of words
trying to make it right...only
the hours that are to come could be so different
knowing the deep stream is flowing between us
where the heart is like a window you push up open,
and the whole bright air is like Spring again.

I'm just ringing because I know more
about the numb silence relationships die in
and because I don't want us to die
a cowardly couple's death

And I'm just ringing because I know
how fleeting it all is, how unbearably brief,
never being as we are in this body again...

Have you turned the sound down ?
Are you call-screening this ?
Will it hang for hours in empty space,
                              awaiting you
with your coating of fine dust from the world ?

And if I had to re-do it all over ?

Just my hand. Just the place
where two souls become as one again
turning air into featherlight flame.

There's nothing else to say.

LULLABY

I love you—sleep.
I love you to the core of your being, sleep.
Little one, sleep.

Listen to the wind.
The wind in the leaves, sleep.
Let the wind breathe, sleep.

Let these arms hold you.
The everlasting arms. Beneath.

And all that the air is, loves you
and all that the wind breathes
whispers to you...

Beloved, child of the spirit, sleep.
Beloved, queen of your heartbeat, sleep.
Beloved, from your head to feet—

Let your mind be sleep.

THE SKY

'Lie back and look up at the sky', you say
after we've finally climbed the hill
where tears of frustration stalled you
enfolded in my arms, aching to be strong;

now you lie back breathing it in from its depth
as I gaze at the cirrus streaks etched high in the blue
back-lit by the crimson yolk of the sun

and spread above us, on the cool autumn grass
with winter closening, as gold turns to twilight
a giant V of cloud, its two branches diverging
but joined in a thickening bole at its base

so as they seemed to be two, they were one
speaking and not speaking, in the silence, at ease
strung like two bow strings, two parentheses in space,
yet from one deep stem, despite everything...

and above it, where the thin wisps flow forward
melding beyond themselves, at the highest,
so that its whole shape becomes a diamond—

is our becoming, that only God knows
and we can only know in as clear a place
that is the space between us where we breathe
and the closeness of our surrender—

so that even as we lie side by side,
back to back, or face to face
even as we live or die

we are still, as secretly, one.

MISSING YOU

The astrochemist is telling us
it's not the stars, but the space between
which generates. Clouds of fine
veiled dust, cocooning
new births of molecules, seeds of everything.

And I am driving back towards an empty house
as space turns into longing, for you...

Stardust as easily pricking into my eyes
as I think of yours, and then see them
flickering in their gaze at mine

and without any feeling I can explain
as tears fill them, becoming ours
at this precise moment—
that is the memory of our knowing, you will say

and is what it means, across all the worlds,
to be able to meet again.

from ANOTHER COUNTRY

for L.

3.

There is a place
of refinement, of full
expression of feeling
where nothing is lost
or forgotten, and everything
can be achieved

It is silver, your face
in a liquid profile
shimmering in its mirror
(part flesh, part metal)
free in its domain
as you need to be, to be
queen of yourself in this coin.

And it is where we're meeting
precious and inclusive
mercurial, permissive
in the dance where we
can be all we are, and more.
We can live our dream.

5.

Dancing all evening
with you inside me
a clear, warm, deep
flame of attention:
what is there to fear ?

You have freed my body
and now there is no one
I can't dare to meet—
my eyes even with loving,
and you are in them

What is between our eyes
in a clear everywhere seeing
all around this circle.
And there is nothing left to fear.
If we could meet each other's eyes

deciding that this was true
there is nothing we could not do.

And we would enter that other country
as surely as it would shine in us
simply as who we've been all along.

13.

What's
the air like
there ?
—Robert Creeley, d. 2004

My hand in your morning,
heart in yours, belly close
I text you, and yet
                          in all this space
we are disembodied, stretched
across the sky towards each other

under the pale apex of the moon
tissue-thin against the blue
above the hill where we will be walking.

Past and future are a dream
but so is this dreaming-you-awake
and is it what it will be like there ?

Only the limitless heart, and a cooling air
as the sun sinks under the horizon behind,
under all the fields I've walked

A cooling infinitude of emerging stars
and yet, beyond all reckoning
you will be so near, arriving...

as its signal suddenly, shrilly bleeps

(And within three minutes, how immediately you are).

14.

Your final surrender,
diving onto the floor as if it was water
so tired you had no energy left
to resist

and so you became the Spirit of the Dance.
And the Spirit gave you animals of itself
an eagle, a snake—and a river
gave as you received

unable to do anything
but be in the picture of your trance.

The Spirit of the Dance danced me.

And in the room, nearly a hundred of you
were all one breathing drum.

It is what we can do together
in that other country where we learn to let go
and pass through a wall of self so thin
we may wonder *was it really there at all ?*

from PEARLS

for L.

22.

Eye to eye, and what it means
to want to come together
as we look into each other's eyes

and what it is, your iris opening
like your mouth like your lips in its silent O
that can gaze and gaze until it feels
this pull to indrawn space

like sleep, but awake
riven with electricity—and it's
like trying to see God, you get
so close with all your heart

and then you have to close your eyes, and let go.

58.

The change that comes
not from the outside, not
from anything observable
but from within: blossoming,
emerging...the subtlest change
that tells us forever
we are more than we know

You and I now
having passed through the fire
learning to love who we are
as tenderly

To be the whole of who we are
within

And knowing the music we play
is the harmony we create—
as sound penetrates water
a dissonant jangle of molecules,
or these star-white crystals.

Love is what we make.

You in your swansdown dressing gown
so like a warm bird to the touch
in our high blue nest room
now frost and freezing mist bites;
learning to hold the light.

68.

How can we fight and yet find
our bodies so close and at peace ?

How can I see you as a stranger,
yet know you as when we first met ?

Is the pain-driven ego so shallow—
bent on blaming and taming
so fully in our faces as it is.
And beneath

our bodies open at peace
our simple bodies, our limbs closening
into their wordless warm embrace...

It is amazing, I tell you
and as I look at how
you've grown together after all these years
etched in counterpoint, in your kindly smiles
of grey and softly wrinkled white
your faces eliding, so nearly the same
in their attentiveness and patience

I see it: being so much
more unconscious than we know
it takes Love to show us what is really real.

69.

How easily broken: our thin filmy
fragile romantic images of each other

in the tideswell and undersurge of the sea
ever-shifting—and suddenly shelving deep

deconstructed in every element
scorched, aerated, immured
                              and yet

they've got to be able to survive it
or else who are we ?

And they're too precious, too sad to be free
to withstand *the jagged rocks of anger
and the well of despair*, as you phrase it—

So they're burnt as we are, immersed
baptized dry again and again,
in the pain we're here to transmute
returning to each other, touched and changed

beyond any single image we could ever have
only your face, now, as it is—

forever in its daily mystery
beyond and within my reach.

92.

May God's love be with you
because it's all there is
that can take us through
beyond our littleness
into the love that gave us
each other in the beginning.

You say there's a God-shaped hole
but I say it's woman-shaped too
you-shaped where only
you are with me—and God is. True.

And it's that which makes us
more than we can be
and not only for each other
but all our extended family;
this Tribe of Love that is
our true community.

May God's love be with you
and it's featherlight, letting you go
to the only place where you're free—
and Love is the space between us.

THE WORDS

for Ann

Right between the eyes, you're telling me
as a fine indented line, a ridged contour
rises from the right side of your forehead—
and in the pauses between where you can't find the words

Blinding light. All I'm seeing. Feinting away from it
the pain of it, again. Almost unimagineable
that dark Cumbrian road, late one winter evening,
and the ice you hit, swerving, skidding, sliding
spelt in slow motion, closening
towards that head-on lorry collision—*oh God*

sitting in this transitory pub garden
perched either side of a deal bench table
shielding our eyes from the June sky's brightness
clouded as it is, as everything hangs

I needed it, I was losing the plot you're saying
as I try to imagine what road you were on
that could have been as dark...letting you speak as you can

wordless as I can be, when I try to write
as if dyslexic, unable to find the right weight
in a blurred pencil drafting—no seeming difference

and with every phrase you find, knowing
that what connects us across time is so much
deeper than any words can finally be anyway

in the felt elastic sense that resonates
blood-warm in its lightning speed between us
and in this tiny space now as we poise, leaning

as far as that endless road I drove to you
North beyond the motorway signs
to where the silhouetted land started to rise
and with the same suspended urgency
for what we shared in your upstairs room
rucking under your duvet, surrendered, wild—

your face so nearly the same, but changed
twelve years on, changeless as you are, as I see
that the pain of it, the turning away
is the sheer life we can't face
that is love, pain, beauty, death, as one, for real

as you fall for a moment into self-comparison
with my life, and hers, as you imagine them
as we name its demon...then there, behind you, look
as we stir to stand: a single mauve poppy
swaying gently on its stem, tissue-light petals rippling, you

your blonde hair grey, eyes blue-sad but singing
as we cross to the other side of the pavement
stretched in our parting to its last glimpse, re-echoed again

Before the same green lanes in reverse
and all the green summers in my heart
that were and are in the heart's own time—

the colour suddenly gleaming, fresh blood between the leaves
pulling over and braking at the sight of two fields
vermilion red with poppies, unbroken, vibrating alive.

AFTER KEATS

for Henry, and Lara

Do you dare ? It has to be yes
her luminous face, blonde hair tied up
aproned, petite, glowing in the restuarant
and your face, your real face
talking about beauty in the gutter
a gravel garden, the smell of dogshit
a bin liner wafting about, a black ghost
(*'if these were your last moments alive, imagine'*)
sometimes beauty and truth, uncooked
seemingly in different worlds.
                                             Or all one world
that cannot be split, but which is
spanned by an indelible rainbow, arcing
from gold to grit, lead to royal purple
soprano to guttural, spitting, clean alpine air
to blue bar-room smoke: it's all here
all true beyond rejection in its place
like each cornerstone of our stories

with an invisible measure we may not discern
(where judgement cannot reach—)
only still feel how truth is beautiful
and beauty truth, if it is true

and not a lie to justify or sell our unbelief.

THE GOLDEN LEAVES

I was in the darkness, Dad
and you were already in the light.

Illuminated in a pool in the dining room
sitting in your usual chair at the head
the dark wooden chair with its arms
at the dark wood table that goes back to the beginning.
Unable to do much of anything now
looking forward, then glancing down
in the reverie that is finally yours, and for you.

I sweep and stoop outside
to the fallen leaves from the balcony creeper
all their spring green turned gold and brown
and tan-gold now; and their stems too
loose as straws, also golden
as the wind breathes, ruffling through them.

I sweep them into a loose pile by the pond's side
before trudging up the inlaid brick path to the shed
to get the leaf collector, and it's then
as I turn back, I see you
wondering if you can see me
sad as this evening late in time
as I gather the golden leaves in the dark
bent with dustpan and brush at last

as you sit as if already in the light.

DRIVING HOME, CHRISTMAS DAY

for my father

You can live half your life in a fantasy of yourself
but suddenly it becomes vital not to lie
about where you came from, and who you are
through those who made you, behind you—
because however difficult they were, they are
your only ground, where the earth bisects
your vertical being and becoming...

Whoever you have behind you, don't discard them
in trying to be yourself; but in seeing them, see
they are the love you have to prove
in this river you've been born into
reaching from your tree into its only roots.

So as I see you sitting in the light and smiling,
in your cream polo kneck, watery blue-eyed, I know
that only the truth allows the love to be
its its shining fullness, allowing me to receive
its strength and blessing, waving me on my way tonight
and every night I'll go on leaving you
to cross this void of darkness outside—

arriving a little deeper into the mystery
of the life that was given to be mine.

THE GOLDEN DANCER

for Polly

Leaf-full, radiant in last light
twilight, red-gold—all at once
the crown a neck, twisted to the left
the arms branches falling at the sides
of a huge sweeping taffetta dress
where they touch the ground, caught in motion
and held there as we become its stillness

perfect in each detail, even to one raised branch
at one side, the equivalent on the other
down-curving as if in a swaying, wafting
of the fabric of the invisible dress
that our eyes see, and see again.

Twilight in Silk Wood—even its name
where everything is possible in Eros
not the main Arboretum with its prescribed trail.
You cut across the paths, knowing another way.
We're talking about her, and her strange liasons,
and then suddenly this magnificent tree
radiant in the twilight—golden dancer...

exactly as we see it, her, at this moment and no other;
as we cross closer to it; and it naturally changes.

Curious, we step around and inside
wanting to name it—beech or alder
as the leaves suggest...and inside its drooping willow-shape
with its surprisingly slender trunk
inside the dancer, her name we find: *Ironwood*
discreetly pinned to the trunk
so you have to change your mind

Persian, strong as her light—

regal as an Angel Prince

embracing the incoming night.

coda

from **DANCES**

7.

Letting go of you
I find you
another you,
another dream

Another meeting
that was meant to be
so many dancers
in one life.

So many dances
and how else
does the music reach us ?
We'd be set in our steps

But the Dance Mistress intervenes
weaving and remixing us again.
How do I know it's you ?
By a light, a luminous

phosphorescence in the human face
glowing with a will of its own
signalling the free
to follow its star.

Star in our hearts
and if we stand in truth
we will never bring
each other harm.

Love is the dance
love in shyness
eros, anger and anguish
and all the unnamed feelings

that entrance us
entering us in always
to our deeper necessity.
Love and this moment

letting go
finding you, and you, and you
until the truth is known:
so many dances, but only One Rose.

NOTES TO THE POEMS

Flower Mountain (Huashan), on the of the big sacred mountain of China, is in Shaanxi Province about 100 miles east of Xian, the old capital.

Kiawah is a small and beautiful holiday island off South Carolina.

The Abbey Garden, Delapre is a suburb of Northampton.

Lina Tegner, a spiritual healer and massage/Rosen therapist living in Stockholm, died in early 2008.

For information about St. Christopher, see A Guide to Hailes Church by Lord Sudeley available from Hailes Abbey National Trust gift shop.

Culbone Church (the smallest parish church in the UK) can be found off the main A39, turning opposite the Culbone Inn, and following the lane on past the Ash Farm turning towards Silcombe Farm. Ash Farm is where Coleridge wrote 'Kubla Khan' in 1798; the Culbone Valley, it seems likely, also appears as 'that steep romantic chasm' just beneath the farm itself.

'Anna O.', her name abbreviated for confidentiality, was one of Freud's original patients, with his colleague Dr. Bruer, from which he developed his questionable theory of hysteria. His own inability to recognize his feelings for her (his countertransference) was part of her demise. Classical psychoanalysis can seem merely 'a countertransference defence against love' (Jarlath Benson); and yet its whole edifice is founded upon the feminine unconscious. That is what this prose-poem noisily celebrates.

The channelled painting referred to in 'Angel of the Inner Ear' was given to me by composer Clement Jewitt in Leicester (2003).

'You' draws on Lesson 10 from Joan Cooper's Cornerstones of the Spiritual World written at Culbone Lodge. Joan (d. 1982) is buried in the graveyard. For further information please apply in writing to Barrie O'Connor at Culbone Lodge, Porlock Weir, Somerset TA24 8PQ—otherwise Jen & Jeff Cox, trustees of her literary estate, on 01643-862959.

'Black Shuck' was written for Janet Bord, co-author (with Colin Bord) of Mysterious Britain.

Shelley lived at Lynmouth with his first wife Harriet Westbrook in 1812. It is now Shelley's Hotel (01598-753219). The reference at the end of the poem is to 'Ode to a Skylark'.

'Anamnesis' from Plato is the opposite of 'amnesia'. It means literally the remembering of what we spiritually know that is encoded within us. This was Plato's idea. In remembering what we know, we remember ourselves.

Montsegur, south of Carcassone in France, is where hundreds of Cathars were murdered as a result of the Albigensian Crusade originally organized by Papal Edict (1324). The Cathars held a vision of a pure Christianity, aligned also to the practise of healing and herbal medicine, and were deeply loved by the French people who did all they could to help them.

ACKNOWLEDGEMENTS

These poems are a selection over 9 years that are drawn from the collection *Midnight Silver* (unpublished, 1997) and bk. 7 of *THE GREAT RETURN*, which is *Via*. This seventh book expands on the structure of 'parallel sequences' which is offered as a framework here.

Some of these poems appeared first in the following magazines and journals: 'Improvisation on Flower Mountain' (*Scintilla*), 'Kiawah' (*Tears in the Fence*), 'The Boreen' (*Scintilla*), 'Spire' (*Acumen*), 'In the North of Sweden' (*Fire*), 'Mdina' (*The London Magazine*), 'from Diary —Iraq poems (*Fire*), 'Fourteen Lines for Britain' (*More to Life*), 'Marathonisi' (*Tears in the Fence*), 'Shapwick' (*Tears in the Fence*), 'A Free Association in the Name of Anna O' (*Tears in the Fence*), 'After Rimbaud' (*Tears in the Fence*), 'A Dream for Easter' (*Scintilla*), 'Getting Through' (*Scintilla*).

Grateful thanks to David Caddy , Anne Cluysenaar, and Jeremy Hilton for their editorial support here.

Some of these poems have also first appeared in *The Message—poems to read the world*, with Karen Eberhardt Shelton (David Paul Books, London, 2002) and *The Heart's Ragged Evangelist—love poems for the greater love* (PSAvalon, 2005). 'A Suicide Bomber Reaches the Light' is part of my contribution to the anthology *Into the Further Reaches—64 Contemporary British Poets and the spiritual journey* (PSAvalon, 2007—also available at www.psavalon.com).

Anamnesis—the remembering of soul was first published as a pamphlet by Revd. Charles Hedley at St James' Church Piccadilly after my 16 month residency (2006) in aid of their Restoration Appeal. The poems were recorded on the CD of that title by Michael Klein for The Lotus Foundation, London (2007), with Tibetan Bowls, available from www. lotusfoundation.org.uk

'*Driving Home, Christmas Day*' was read at my father Donald Ramsay-Brown's memorial service at The Church of St Nicholas, Islip, Oxon. on 25.7.07.—in his 90th year. For the strength of his spirit, beyond time now, belonging also in a world within this world, inside, only the best I can make of my own life is enough.

Special thanks to Martin Palmer, Genie Poretsky-Lee at The Lotus Foundation (my London poetry group), Maxine Relton (my Gloucestershire poetry group), Donna Salisbury, Mary Gold, Polly Howell, Carole Bruce, Lara Fiedler, and Will Parfitt/PSAvalon for taking this on for my 50th in time.

PS AVALON PUBLISHING

About PS Avalon

PS Avalon Publishing is an independent and committed publisher offering a complete publishing service. As a small publisher able to take advantage of the latest technological advances, PS Avalon Publishing can offer an alternative route for aspiring authors in our particular fields of interest.

As well as publishing, we offer an education programme including courses, seminars, group retreats, and other opportunities for personal and spiritual growth. Whilst the nature of our work means we engage with people from all around the world, we are based in Glastonbury which is in the West Country of England.

new poetry books

Our purpose is to bring you the best new poetry with a psychospiritual content, work that is contemplative and inspirational, with a dark, challenging edge.

self development books

We publish inspiring reading material aimed at enhancing your personal and spiritual development in which everything is kept as simple and as accessible as possible.

PS AVALON PUBLISHING
Box 1865, Glastonbury,
Somerset BA6 8YR, U.K.
www.psavalon.com
info@psavalon.com

Lightning Source UK Ltd.
Milton Keynes UK
UKOW050510161011

180370UK00001B/52/P